Titans

of the

Forests

The Economic Evolution
of the Human Species
and that of Our Cultures

Gregory V. Short

VERNON PRESS

This book is dedicated to all of the men and women,

who will pause during their hectic day of survival

and look up into the clear blue sky

and wonder.

---

www.vernonpress.com

In the Americas:
Vernon Press
1000 N West Street,
Suite 1200, Wilmington,
Delaware 19801
United States

In the rest of the world
Vernon Press
C/Sancti Espiritu 17,
Malaga, 29006
Spain

Library of Congress Control Number: 2014942085

ISBN 978-1-62273-037-7

Contents

Prologue

Ever since I was a college student, I have always been fascinated with the many different theories that have attempted to explain our astonishing development as a species. Within the scientific community, the world's biologists, anthropologists, archaeologists, geneticists, paleontologists, and zoologists have written enough material on the subject by to have filled a library. As a group, they have literally dragged us into the 21th century when it comes to understanding the origin and the physical development of our species. And yet within each of these specialized fields of study, their research has encompassed only one of the many facets of the evolutionary process. As a matter of fact, the subject of our evolution has become so fragmented into the different overlapping fields of study that evolution itself has come to mean many different things to many different people. In a very real sense, the scientists are so far into the trees that they have actually ignored the forest. Consequently, we teach human evolution as a hodgepodge of different theories within the realm of microevolution, thus failing to understand or even to recognize the economic thread that binds them altogether.

Over the past century, our scientists and scholars have continuously disagreed over what particular characteristics or abilities have separated us as a species from the rest of the animal kingdom. And just when a scientist believes that he or she has found a significant difference between us, someone else discovers a species that also possesses the same ability. As the volume of research increases, it has become apparent that we have more in common with the other creatures around us than we would like to admit. As a matter of fact, our ability to communicate and organize ourselves, to learn and reason, to use tools, and to build structures is not unique. Even though we have developed these skills to a very high degree, many other species in the world have also exhibited these same abilities. However, there can be no denying the fact that there is a big difference.

Instead of dwelling on the biological, physiological, or even the genetic aspects of our evolution, I have taken a completely different approach which could be referred to as the unchartered and neglected field of macroevolution. It is my contention that we as a species were initially forced to change our way of obtaining nourishment, or rather our various economies, in order to adapt to the ever-changing world. And as a result of this economic adaptation, our species would then and only then begin to change into our present form. *In other words, our species' biological, physiological, psychological, and cultural evolution has been instigated, propelled, and shaped by our economic adaptation to a fluctuating environment.* Of course, this is not a new concept by any means. In the past, a few scholars and scientists have written about it. But to my knowledge, it never has been fully explored as the "central theme" to our evolution.

It has been widely acknowledged by the scientific community that we evolved from a lower form of primate species, specifically a predecessor of the chimpanzee. And yet as we slowly evolved into our present physical form; our economies along with our societies have also evolved with us. Undoubtedly, these parallel developments weren't by mere happenstance.

Throughout our incredible evolution, our earliest economies have not only instigated our physical development, but they have also helped form the institutional framework of our societies. While being more than just a mere system of production and consumption, a society's economy will shape our cultural values, traditions, behavioral patterns, and our social structure. Moreover, it will determine the formation of our institutions, the composition of our ruling bodies, the type of technologies we employ, the size and configuration of our families, the methods in which we fight our wars, and even the way we perceive and worship our deities. As a matter of fact, the type of economy we employ influences almost every aspect of our lives.

By reexamining our prehistoric past, I will be describing our species' early economic evolution, along with the environmental forces that have helped shaped us. It is not my intention to form a judgment about the different scientific controversies surrounding our evolution, such as the "Out of Africa" versus the "Multiregional" theory or whether or not the Homo ergaster and the Homo erectus were really the same species. Even though these are very important issues, they are not at all relevant towards describing our economic evolution.

What we do know with a high degree of certainty is that our primate ancestors dwelled in the forests of eastern Africa approximately 5 million years ago as four-legged, tree-dwelling food gatherers. Then later as the earth's climate began to cool in successive shifts and the dense forests became smaller, they were forced to move out into the surrounding savannas, where eventually they evolved into two-legged, ground-inhabiting scavengers. Over the next 3.3 million years, our species would progressively become nomadic hunters, farmers and herders, and then ultimately industrial, financial, bureaucratic, and technological workers. And within that same period, we would proceed through what is commonly known as the Stone, Bronze, and Iron Ages, while eventually reaching the Nuclear Age.

As an educator with almost forty years of experience, I have studied many different societies in our long history, along with their different economies. Very early in my career, I began to realize that our earliest economies (food gathering, scavenging, and nomadism) had evolved much like our own species. By comparing my accumulated knowledge about our earliest economies with that of the popular scientific literature that pertains to our physical and biological evolution, I came to the conclusion that they were directly interrelated. Thus, I began to integrate the timeline of our prehistoric past to that of our earliest economies. As a result, I was able to synthesize a sequence of events that illustrates the relationship between our economic and physical evolution.

Considering that I am not a scientist, this book is not intended to be a scientific study. For much too long, the world's scientific community has directed the discussion of our incredible evolution. In point of fact, our biological and physiological development has been but a derivative of our economic evolution. For unlike the rest of the animal kingdom, we possess the extraordinary ability to change our economy, which has made us an extremely adaptable species.

Unfortunately, the overwhelming majority of the scholarly works about our prehistoric past have been based upon speculative conjecture and this book isn't any different. However, it was my intention to describe for the first time how we survived and evolved by altering our economies in response to the earth's changing climate, thus creating a systematic and holistic approach in revealing the economic basis of our remarkable ascension.

Many of my facts about our beginnings will be open for discussion, because much what we know about our prehistoric ancestors has been based upon the interpretation of their very few scattered remains and artifacts. Thus, the accumulated knowledge, as we know it today, is always changing in the light of new discoveries. Therefore, it is my earnest hope that this working model will encourage others to further explore the tremendous impact our economic adaptation has had upon our physical and cultural evolution.

Gregory V. Short

Introduction

While revolving around an enormously bright sun amid scores of planets, moons, comets, and asteroids, our planet has experienced many different climatic changes in its 4.5 billion years of existence. The gradual changes of the earth's axis, the movements of the continents, the uplifting of the mountains, the shifting of the ocean's currents, or even a sudden catastrophic event have all had a profound effect upon our planet's surface and the life forms that reside here. Thus, the evolution of life has been predicated upon the constant change of the earth's environment and the incredible ability of its organisms to adapt to those changes.

Generally speaking, a species does not just randomly change for the sake of change. As the earth's unpredictable climate changes toward any particular direction, no matter how slightly, it will either adapt to meet those changes or it will begin to face extinction. These changes in the environment have manifested themselves in many different ways and in many different time spans. For instance, a subtle change in the earth's temperature, a change in the level of rainfall, or even a sudden change in the course of a river can all have far reaching affects upon the development of a species. In other words, the most minuscule change in a species' environment can alter the way in which it can subsist.

Of course, despite the major changes in our environment, there exist many different species of animals, insects, and fish that have remained the same for eons of time. Their successful adaptation was due to them reproducing a significant number of offspring that have possessed the most beneficial biological traits towards ensuring their long term survival.

Through the process of natural selection, organisms (species) have slowly branched out (speciation) in a step by step progression (gradualism) as they formed new and sometimes more complex organisms within their own particular location. As a result, the subgroup of a particular species that possesses the best suited characteristics for adapting to its changing environment will leave behind the most descendants of that species, thus ensuring its survival and genetic continuation. Unfortunately through, a species can become extinct for a variety of reasons. However, their eventual extinction will pave the way for a new species to emerge in order to occupy their previous ecological niche.

In general, the physical evolution of a species is predicated upon its biological adaptation and successful reproduction of its offspring. In contrast, the cultural evolution of a human society is predicated upon its economic adaptation and the successful continuation of its people and their culture. Both are living, struggling, and organic organisms whose survival is dependent upon their ability to adapt and then multiply within any given environment.

Much like our biological evolution, human societies have also branched out in a gradual progression by forming more complex civilizations through the processes of natural selection. Whereupon, the societies that developed the best-suited economic characteristics for adapting have had a better chance for survival than the societies that possessed the least-suited characteristics. This does not mean that the cruelest and the most ruthless or the most powerful society will survive as the popular term "the survival of fittest" mistakenly implies. But rather, the society that is the most economically adaptable during the times of adversity will inevitably leave behind the most cultural offspring in terms of its institutions, organizational methods, traditions, and its wealth. In other words, the human society that fails to economically adapt to its changing environment will find itself becoming extinct or absorbed into another civilization (acculturation).

Whenever a human society is confronted with environmental changes, it can also mutate into another form of society in much the same manner as a species can mutate into another species. This form of mutation will initially occur when a society begins to change its economy in an effort to adapt. Our earliest known societies were classic examples of cultures that had successfully mutated from a nomadic to an agrarian economy. After settling down along the world's great river systems, our wandering ancestors would begin to domesticate the plants and animals, whereby eventually forming villages, digging canals, and constructing roads as a byproduct of their developing farms. Although, these farming communities were springing up all over the world, they still displayed the same cultural traits exhibited by all farming societies. With the mutation of their economies, these societies would be inevitably transformed into a completely different culture; much like a species is transformed into a different species.

It is by no mere coincidence that every major evolutionary and economic transmutation experienced by our prehistoric ancestors has occurred after the earth has experienced a climatic shift. Beginning almost 5 million years ago, the earth was already becoming cooler and drier then the previously warm and moist Miocene Epoch. As the forests in eastern Africa began to slowly shrink into a sea of grass, the first known hominids (Australopithecus afarensis) would suddenly appear around 3.7 million years ago. Forced to move out of their habitats, these "Titans of the Forests" challenged Mother Nature and ultimately ventured out onto the vast savannas to find food and shelter within the isolated canyons and arroyos. Secure in their new environment, they would continue to gather food and hunt the smaller game in the same manner as their ancestors before them.

Then around 3.3 million years ago, the Australopithecus africanus/ garhi suddenly appeared. More apelike than human, these australopithecines were more skillful with their hands, erect in their posture, and more mobile than that of their A. afarensis predecessors. But more importantly, as a result of learning how to survive on the savannas, they would become increasingly more carnivorous in their eating habits by beginning to scavenge the surrounding carcasses.

With the beginning of the "Great Pleistocene Ice Age," the first distinctive human (Homo habilis) species made their appearance a little over 2 million years ago. As a group, they weren't physically or socially developed enough to permanently move out into the savannas. But they were capable enough to become successful scavengers. While possessing the ability to make crude tools and the capacity for rudimentary communication, these bipedal (two-legged) creatures were able to temporarily trek out into the savannas and scavenge the remains of carcasses. Even though they had a larger brain then their australopithecine cousins and possessed a greater flexibility in their hands, which were capable of performing precise grips, they would become extinct soon after the rise of another human species.

Approximately 1.8 million years ago, the Homo ergaster/erectus suddenly emerged and began to develop a whole new human economy (nomadic). As a consequence of their predecessor's physical adaptation of living as scavengers, they slowly migrated out of Africa and into Eurasia. As a result of their long journeys, these nomadic hunters had become fairly human-like in their appearance, socially organized, and very well-armed. Existing for an incredibly long time, these highly mobile hunters would form our first family units and begin to initiate the early foundations of our present day institutions.

It was during this period that the earth had been oscillating between the colder and dryer glacial periods to the warmer and moister interglacial periods. Lasting up to 100,000 years at a time, the glacial periods were dominated by a continuous increase in the size of the polar glaciers, a shrinking of the world's oceans, lakes, and rivers, prolonged droughts, and the appearance of land bridges between the continents. On the other hand, the warmer and moister interglacial periods, which last approximately 15,000 to 30,000 years at a time, were characterized by a receding of the glaciers back to their poles, an increase in the rainfall, global flooding, and an explosion of plant and animal life.

At the peak of the last glaciation period, approximately 18,000 years ago, the massive herds of roaming animals were beginning to become extinct as a consequence in the decrease of the worldwide vegetation and the over-hunting by the nomads. As a response to the lack of game, our nomadic ancestors that hadn't already crossed the Bering Strait into North America would begin to adapt to the changing environment by developing a new economy (agrarian). Thus, the domestication of plants and animals just didn't randomly occur approximately 11,500 years ago. Much like our Homo ergaster/erectus ancestors that had been forced out of Africa and compelled to become nomadic, we would begin to consciously establish a new economy (agrarianism) as a direct response to a changing world.

Of course, the earth's changing environment isn't the only reason why we were able to develop several new economies. There were many other factors at work as well that have made it possible. Our continuous physical, biological, and cultural adaptations, along with our expanding technological, organizational, communication, and cognitive skills were all very important aspects of our evolution. However, none of these factors would have become crucial, if our primeval ancestors had lived on an unchanging planet.

Prehistoric humans were physically, mentally, and culturally quite similar to present-day humans. The similarities between us far outweigh our differences in terms to our reaction to each other and to the environment. It would be a grave mistake by anyone to perceive these early humans as something less than human. In fact, they were quite human. Very little is actually known about their belief systems, but what can be surmised is that they physically, emotionally, and mentally struggled for their survival. They formed and cherished their families, organized their groups, created tools and weapons, coveted their possessions, cried over their dead, and looked up into the night sky in astonishment. Physically, they were awkward, dirty, and haggard. But among their scattered remains, lies the genesis of human civilization - a genesis that has led us to the splitting of the atom and the venturing out into outer space.

As a species, we have evolved into a very complex and gifted creature. We are the builders of cities and nations, the recorders of knowledge and history, and the pioneers of the unknown and beyond. Yet above all else, we have become creatures of exploitation and domination. What success we have achieved has been founded upon our ability to overcome immense adversity by economically adapting to an ever-changing world by the simple exploitation of everything around us. Within our own remarkable economic development, we have endeavored to dominate every aspect of our surroundings, including time, space, and the elements. Thus, the very essence of ourselves and that of our societies has been rooted and forged by the combination of our uncommon exploitive and dominant nature, and the economies we have created.

In the past 5 million years, our societies have also evolved and become more technologically advanced. Yet paradoxically, the age-old human dilemmas of providing food, shelter, and defense for our families hasn't changed since we initially left the primeval forests of eastern Africa. While these dilemmas have remained constant throughout our past, the economic solutions to these dilemmas have periodically changed as our economies have changed. Even today, the rise of modern science and technology may have altered the way in which we live, but they haven't changed our indigenous nature nor have they changed the dilemmas themselves. Faced with the ever-growing economic problem of "scarcity" (limited resources versus unlimited demand), we have always reacted to any environmental threat to our existence by forming new economies and thus new cultures. As a matter of fact, it is this unique ability to deliberately change our economy that has separated us from the rest of the animal kingdom. As an evolutionary response to a changing world, we have been able to successfully adapt, while many other species have failed.

The struggle for human survival has been ruthless, unforgiving, and even heroic in our endeavor to exist. For over the span of time, we have roamed throughout the vastness of the globe in an attempt to feed our families, safe guard our homes, and to secure a better future for our children. Amid the scattered wreckage and the hallowed monuments of our success, we have exemplified a spirit of ceaseless determination, underlying imagination, unbridled aggressiveness, and boundless energy. And yet within these same admirable and ambivalent traits rests either the seeds of our continued survival or that of our premature extinction. Only time will tell.

Chapter One
The Dawn
"The Rise of Mammals"

"The reason why the universe is eternal is that it does not live for itself. Instead, it gives life to others as it transforms."

Lao Tzu (570-490 B.C.)
Chinese Taoist Philosopher

At the end of the Cretaceous Period, approximately 65 million years ago, the earth's two supercontinents were in the process of slowly breaking apart into the seven continents that we know of today. Commonly known as Laurasia and Gondwanaland, they had previously formed a huge landmass called Pangaea, which had extended from end of the globe to the other. Overall, it had been a relatively unstable period characterized by an increase of volcanic activity and the movement of the continental plates. The sea levels were high and covered much of the earth's continental shelves, which had produced a swampy heaven for the indigenous dinosaurs. The climate was generally warm and tropical with an abundance of rainfall that gave sustenance to its diverse plant life. A wide variety of coniferous and deciduous trees had been growing and prospering in the ice-free Polar Regions, where the temperatures had remained warm. With the absence of permafrost, the animals had been free to roam from continent to continent without any interference from the weather.[1]

In the Northern Hemisphere, the supercontinent of Laurasia was in the process of breaking apart into the continents of Eurasia and North America, thus forming the North Atlantic Ocean. Greenland was still connected to North America as they slowly moved westward, leaving the island of Iceland behind in their wake. Meanwhile, the Southern Hemisphere's continental plates of Gondwanaland were continuing to shift with the expansion of the oceans' floor. The continent of Africa was slowly drifting away from the clutches of South America and moving northwards towards Europe, thus eventually halting and forming the southern shores of the Mediterranean Sea. While possessing the same type of flora and wildlife, the continents of Australia and Antarctica were still temporarily locked together. However, the land mass of modern day India had already broken away from their shorelines and was headed towards a massive collision with southern Asia. This collision would ultimately push up the Himalayan Mountain ranges and the majestic cliffs of the Tibetan Plateau.[2]

As the deep blue oceans gave rise to an abundance of coral reefs and marine life, a multitude of archipelagoes began springing up from the depths of the oceans' floor as a succession of powerful volcanoes exploded and spewed their hot magma high into the atmosphere. By and large, the oceans were filled with an amazing assortment of marine life. Ammonites such as the octopus, squid, and the cuttlefish strived amid the reef-building organisms called rudists. However prowling beneath the oceans' waves were extremely deadly reptilian predators. Agile for their size and snake-like in their appearance, the Mosasaurs and the Plesiosaurs were the largest creatures ever to swim the oceans, long before the whales had even appeared.[3]

For almost 135 million years up to the end the Cretaceous Period, the dinosaurs reigned supreme among the rain forests and thick plush jungles. Referred to as the "Age of Reptiles," these extremely versatile creatures dominated the earth as no other species before or after them. While roaming the land or soaring through the open skies, they formed a highly complex food chain that encompassed an extensive array of ferocious carnivores and docile herbivores. Idolized by the contemporary movies, the most commonly known dinosaurs were quite large, aggressive, and very agile. And yet, the overwhelmingly majority of them were much smaller than the average deer. Ranging in size from the enormous 100 ton Argentinosaurus to the minuscule Microraptor, which weighed less than 10 pounds apiece, they were tremendously adaptable creatures when it came to moving into a new territory. Today, modern scientists have identified and named well over 1000 different species of reptiles. And yet incredibly, these same scientists believe that they have only discovered the remains of about one quarter of the ones that had actually existed.[4]

It was during this same time that many forms of modern plants, invertebrates, and marine life had also come into existence. As the continents continued to drift away from each other, the animal and plant life began to develop their own regional differences. Producing a wide variety of complex ecosystems, these residing life forms were able to blossom into many different mutually-dependent branches. And even though there was a tremendous amount of tectonic and climatic activity across the surface of the earth, the indigenous flowering plants (angiosperms) and the insects would continue to spread and become even more diversified as they benefited from each other's presence.[5]

Then without any warning, an extraordinary and awe-inspiring astronomical event occurred that today's scientists are still investigating. Incredibly, it would suddenly and irreversibly throw our planet into a whole new geological (Cenozoic) era by eradicating the overwhelming majority of the species on earth. Devastating in its impact and horrifying in its aftereffects, it initiated a series of catastrophe events of such gigantic proportions that they would ultimately eliminate the non-avian dinosaurs and propel the evolution of a whole new array of species, including that of our own primate ancestors.[6]

Around 65 million years ago, a huge fiery asteroid came plummeting through the earth's atmosphere at the speed of approximately 20 kilometers (12 miles) per second, hitting the eastern coastline of the Yucatan peninsula in present day Mexico. Known as the K-Pg extinction event that established the Cretaceous Tertiary geological boundary, the ensuing massive explosion sent its rocky debris soaring high into the stratosphere, whereupon producing a crater (Chicxulub) approximately 180 kilometers (111.8 miles) wide and 20 kilometers (12 miles) deep. According to the measurements of the crater, the size of the asteroid has been estimated to have been 10 kilometers (6.2 miles) in diameter and weighing close to 1,000 billion tons. Upon impact, scientists have estimated that it produced the equivalent explosion of 100 million tons of TNT, which is more than 10,000 times explosive energy than the combined nuclear arsenals possessed during the Cold War.[7]

Soon afterwards as the fiery fragments reentered the earth's atmosphere, they ignited a series of fires that stretched across the width and breadth of the continents. Within a short period of time, the earth's heavily vegetated landmasses would become an inferno of gale force winds and raging firestorms, thus leaving behind a wasteland of burnt out forests, barren mountains, and desolate river valleys.[8]

As a result of the raising smoke from the firestorms and the lingering debris from the massive explosion, the sun's rays were unable to penetrate the atmosphere. Creating an eerie period of darkness throughout the entire planet for possibly up to a year, the remaining populations of animal life that had survived the blast, the earthquakes, and the firestorms were even further reduced by the lack of sun light and the eventual greenhouse effect that followed.[9]

In the aftermath, the previously diverse plant life almost completely disappeared from the landscapes, whereby severely decreasing the herbivores' ability to find enough food to sustain them. Then once the large herbivores had begun to fall, the carnivores would soon follow. It has been estimated that approximately 70% of the land and marine animals were unable to survive the succession of catastrophes. With many of them weighing more than 55 pounds apiece, these large vertebrates had found themselves caught in harm's way, due to their cumbersome size and their even larger appetites.[10]

Almost immediately following the smoldering devastation and the darkness that preceded it, the archaeological record indicates that the dinosaurs had suddenly disappeared from the face of the earth. Of course, there are several other theories as to the their unexpected demise, including a change in the climate due to the continental drifts, an increase in the earth's volcanic activity (Deccan Traps), the effects of disease and starvation, or the appearance of egg-eating mammals. But as the present evidence strongly indicates, the asteroid and its lethal aftereffects were probably the main culprits behind their final extinction.[11]

After the K-Pg impact, the first modern rain forests began to appear with their towering canopies and thick undergrowth. Teeming with an incredible assortment of plant life, these virgin forests would spring up along the equator and enrich the atmosphere with their oxygen. As a consequence, an evolutionary explosion, or rather a radiation of animal life, began to occur among the humid dense forests and green jungles. Recognized as the "Age of Mammals," the ensuing Cenozoic Era is also known for a tremendous growth and development of the earth's birds, marine, and plant life. Cranes, hawks, ducks, owls, pelicans, and pigeons began to appear in the open skies and multiply in great numbers. While in the surrounding oceans, the ever-restless sharks replaced the giant marine reptiles as the top predators of the deep. However just by their sheer numbers and astonishing diversity, it was the mammals that would replace the dinosaurs and come to dominate the earth's land surfaces.[12]

Occupying the same ecological niches left behind by the extinction of the dinosaurs, the once obscure small, rodent-like mammals began to flourish within the towering trees, thick vines, and dense underbrush of these untamed paradises. As possible descendants of synapsids (mammal-like reptiles), the overall majority of these warm-blooded creatures weren't much larger than a modern day weasel. Along with having an elongated furry body, four short legs, and a triangular-shaped head, they possessed a long narrow snout and a set of large oval shaped eyes. Free to multiply amid this plush environment of few predators, mammals such as the Periptychus, Dissacus, Pantolambda, Claenodon, and the Psittacotherium would all thrive within a literal Garden of Eden without ever having to experience the ecological pressures to adapt.[13]

Born alive and then nurtured on their mother's milk, these mammals were predominately nocturnal creatures that consumed a wide variety of insects, eggs, and plants. Even though a large number of them dwelled on the forests' soggy floor, several of the species maintained their habitats in the surrounding trees. Overall, they were an extremely resilient and adaptable species that over time flourished in almost every kind of environment. Among the dense jungles of the tropics, the vast green forests of the highlands, and the shifting sands of the deserts, they spent their nights searching for food, until the approaching dawn forced them to find sanctuary within their secluded dens. But for the ones in the East African rain forests that were adaptable enough to have survived the Paleocene-Eocene Thermal Maximum, a period of extreme global warming approximately 55 million years ago, one of their distance tree-dwelling descendants would one day rise up from the dense forests and roam the earth as early humans.[14]

At the beginning of the Oligocene Epoch approximately 34 million years ago, the earth's climate began to slowly change in response to a couple of geological factors. The continued ascension of the world's largest mountain ranges such as the Himalayas, the Alps, and the Andes slowly decreased the level of carbon dioxide in the atmosphere, thus reducing the greenhouse effect that had previously warmed the earth's circulating air. Meanwhile, the continents of South America, Australia, and Antarctica were slowly separating from each other, hence creating the Antarctic Circumpolar Current, which ultimately cooled the earth's oceans and helped form the Antarctic ice cap. As a result, the earth's surface began to experience a long period of global cooling. The previously giant forests and humid jungles would begin to shrink and become surrounded by a sea of golden grasslands (savannas).[15]

Oddly enough, the expansion and growth of these grasses had a tremendous impact upon our evolution. Forced to either abandon the shrinking forests or to face starvation, a large number of the mammals began to migrate out onto these newly formed grasslands, whereby discovering a whole new habitat for them to roam and find nourishment. High in fiber and low in protein, these hardy plants had become so abundant that over the next several million years, a multitude of hoofed mammals began to appear and multiply in great numbers, eventually forming vast herds of grazing herbivores. As predecessors of today's wildebeests, gazelles, rhinos, giraffes, camels, and horses, these mammals would one day provide the needed nutrition for our later-day nomadic ancestors. However with the appearance of these herbivores, a wide range of carnivores such as the forerunners of the ferocious lions, cheetahs, bears, hyenas, and leopards would also eventually appear on the savannas in search of fresh meat. Together, they had established a whole new and fully developed eco-system.[16]

Through the processes of natural selection and mutation, this transition of evolving from one species into another must have taken several million years. Incredibly though, before they had finally become extinct, several of the species that had moved out onto the savannas would eventually grow into unbelievably huge and powerful creatures. Besides the domineering presence of the massive Deinotherium (elephant-like) and the Arsinotheres (rhino-like), there was the Indricotherium, an animal estimated at having been 18 feet tall and weighing around 20 tons.[17]

Yet for the mammals that had stayed behind in the thick forests, they also slowly evolved into an assortment of different animals as they adapted to the changing circumstances. These remaining mammals began to diversify into a wide array of new species by filling the vacant niches of those animals that had immigrated out into the savannas. Rodents, porcupines, guinea pigs, a variety of big cats, and of course monkeys, would all thrive within an isolated environment that protected them from the harsh elements.

It was during the early Miocene Epoch, approximately 23 million years ago, that the anthropoid apes sprang forth and began gathering food within the tropical rain forests of eastern Africa. As a subgroup of the prosimians (primitive primates), which includes lemurs, lorises, tarsiers, tree shrews, pottos, and galagos, this new species of tree-dwelling primates would eventually branch out and develop into a diverse collection of chimpanzees, gorillas, orangutans, and gibbons. As robust and comparatively large creatures, they possessed a set of grasping (prehensile) hands and feet, opposable thumbs and toes, a bowed spine, rotating shoulder joints, and stereoscopic vision (depth perception). Yet besides possessing these unique physical characteristics, they also had a fairly large mammalian brain (400cc) that consisted of layers of neocortex (gray matter), which would make them an extremely shrewd and adaptable species.[18]

Over time, our anthropoid ancestors were able to adapt to the heavily vegetated environment by the mutual stimulation of their innate physical and mental abilities. This bilateral stimulation between their physical and mental abilities probably began as a result of them being forced from the trees and onto the ground in order to seek out more nourishment. By employing their grasping hands, stereoscopic vision, and their ability to temporarily to move around on their two legs, they were able to supplement their diets by periodically killing and then consuming the flesh of small animals. While becoming more carnivorous and less nocturnal in their feeding habits, they were able to slowly push themselves up the food chain. As a result, this new source of protein not only helped to further develop their mental abilities, but it also helped to stimulate the necessity to better organize their species, so that they could obtain more protein. Intelligent, aggressive, and group orientated, these extraordinarily restless creatures would stake out their territories and begin laying claim to the vast forests and jungles in eastern Africa.[19]

Unfortunately, we know very little about them. Unlike the more recent australopithecines (southern apes), these earlier anthropoid primates dwelled almost exclusively in the dense forests, where fossilization doesn't readily occur. Hence what information we do have about them has come from the studies of our nearest living relative in the animal kingdom, the chimpanzee. By using modern genetic techniques, the scientific community has discovered that the chromosome comparison between ourselves and that of the chimpanzee is closer (94% to 97%) than it is with any other creature of the animal kingdom. Whether we like it or not, our lineage is directly linked to them. However up to this point, it still isn't clear which of the early anthropoids we can actually call our forefathers and mothers.[20]

There is archaeological evidence that several different species of apes, such as the Morotopithecus, Nyanzapithecus, Afropithecus, Heliopithecus, Kenyapithecus, Griphopithecus, Otavipithecus, Dryopithecus, Choroapithecus, Samburupithecus, Graecopithecus, Nakalipithecus, Oreopithecus, and the Lufengpithecus species existed in between 8 to 20 million years ago. Even though very few remains of these creatures have been discovered, one of them could have been the last common ancestor (LCA), or rather the "missing link," the same ancestral ape that we had with the chimpanzee.[21]

Then there are the Sahelanthropus tchadensis, Orrorin tugenensis, and the Ardipithecus ramidus/kadabba apes that appeared from 4.5 to 7 million years ago. Since their discoveries, it is believed that one of these species of apes might have been our direct ancestors. Considering that they are all excellent candidates, there hasn't been enough physical remains unearthed to conclusively prove that they were a part of our family tree. All that is positively known about our past ascension is that we are related to the common chimpanzees and that we diverged from the same species of anthropoid primate as far back as 6 million years ago or maybe even longer.[22]

Several of today's scientists and scholars have theorized that our primate ancestors were a special type of ape. In that, they started out as creatures quite different from the other apes. Some of them believe that we actually came from a group of predominately ultra-violent (killer) apes that had arisen from the shadowy forests of Africa to eventually wreak havoc across the great savannas. While many other researchers believe that we evolved from a unique group of apes that were extraordinarily intelligent, organized, and cooperative. And that they were eventually forced to become aggressive, predominately carnivorous scavengers in order to survive the open plains. Then there is another group of researchers that believes our ancestors evolved from a group of apes that were very similar to our chimpanzee cousins. In that they were not only instinctively aggressive, but that they were also fairly intelligent, communal, and territorial creatures, whose ability to adapt within a changing environment would eventually enable them to evolve into modern humans.[23]

Undoubtedly, every one of these very distinctive qualities and genetic differences were essential to our evolution. Although, it does beg the question as to whether or not our primate ancestors were really all that special. Unbeknownst to the average person, there were quite a few distinctively different hominids that had also existed long before and even among our own hominid ancestors.

Besides the six known species of australopithecines, the Kenyanthropus platyops, and the Paranthropus branch of hominids, modern scientists have also discovered the Homo ergaster, H.

gautengensis, H. habilis, H. rudolfensis, H. georgicus, and the numerous Homo erectus' subspecies such as the Homo erectus pithecanthropus, H. e. lantianensis, H. e. palaeojavanicus, H. e. yuanmouensis, H. e. wushanensis, H. e. nankinensis, H. e. tautavelensis, and the H. e. soloensis. Then there is the Homo pekinensis, H. cepranensis, H. antecessor (mauritanicus), H. heidelbergensis (rhodesiensis), H. Helmei, and the early Homo sapiens, along with the Homo sapiens sapiens and their subspecies, such as the Denisovans, the H. s. neanderthalensis, the H. s. floresiensis, and H. s. sapiens idaltu.[24]

Hence, it is quite possible that some of them may not have been a part of our family tree, and that they had originated from a completely different branch of anthropoid primates. And if this is the case, which is a real possibility, then our evolution may not have been as unique as we would like to believe. Until more of their remains can be discovered, this controversial question won't be entirely answered. But whatever the final verdict, it would have taken a very aggressive, intelligent, and determined group of creatures to have climbed down from the safety of the trees and to have consciously altered their eating habits, or rather their economy towards scaveging.[25]

As a result of becoming scavengers, and then later nomads, our primate ancestors' physical and mental development were strikingly enhanced and even propelled by the change in the way they obtained their sustenance. Eventually becoming totally erect in their movements, their brains would steadfastly become larger and more complex as they moved farther out onto the savannas and became more carnivorous in their eating habits. Meanwhile, their hands eventually became so skillful that their later-day descendants would one day become the creators of symbols, the makers of weapons and tools, and the builders of shelters. But even more significantly, they were also forced out of pure necessity to adapt to their changing economy by becoming more proficient in their verbal, social, and reasoning skills in order to survive the harsh realities of a brave new world.

Needless to say, the development of these different types of skills had a snowball effect upon our evolution by ultimately enabling our ancestors' offspring to form other and more productive economies. Still and all, there are many remaining questions and uncertainties in the scientific and academic communities as to why our species has continued to evolve, while the other primates appear to be locked in time. Presently, they can be observed in their few remaining habitats and in the zoos all around the world. So why did our ancestors continue to evolve, while the rest of the primates have appeared to have remained locked in time?

Clearly not all of the primates in eastern Africa were forced out of their wooded habitats around 5 million years ago. Once the climate had begun to change, it was only within the smaller woodlands that the various species of primates would find themselves in desperate need to move out onto the savannas. By their sheer size, the larger woodlands were able to maintain a significant number of primates without disrupting their food chain. Consequently, the primates that had stayed behind in the larger primordial forests have basically remained the same, because they continued to occupy the same ecological niches as that of their ancestors. Hence, their physical and mental adaptation weren't stimulated to any great degree by the need to change their habitats or their eating habits (economy).[26]

However, the food gathering primates that did venture out of the forests were able to change their eating habits, or rather their economy to one of scavenging. In doing so, they abandoned their ancestors' ecological niches of the forests by becoming even more mobile (erect) and carnivorous. Then once they had successfully adapted to becoming scavengers, approximately 2 million years ago, the environment would begin to change again.[27]

In response to these environmental changes, our scavenging ancestors were forced to permanently move out onto the savannas. Thus as a consequence of changing their economy, they would in time physically, mentally, and socially adapt to becoming full-time nomads. Although, they would become progressively more carnivorous, their band's survival wasn't based upon which of them was the meanest, the cruelest, or even the most bloodthirsty. Instead, it was based upon which of them were the most adaptable, mobile, organized, and able to reproduce a large number of offspring. For when our ancestors had left the dense forests, their struggle for survival was no longer exclusively based upon the fittest or even the strongest. The rules of the game had unknowingly changed within their new nomadic economy. The nomads that could operate as an efficient coordinated group of skilled hunters and were mobile and daring enough to move to greener pastures would possess a clear advantage over those that couldn't.[28]

Essentially, our species' evolution was initiated by a combination of global events that were directly related to the ever-changing environment. In the absence of any one of these environmental factors, our primate ancestors would still be living among trees with the chimpanzees. Once the earth's environment had slowly become cooler and drier, it created a chain reaction of events that would change the face of Africa. Besides the emergence of the various types of grasses on the ever-growing savannas and the eventual appearance of a multitude of grazing and predatory mammals, the periodic shrinking of the African forests would drive our ancestors out into the vast savannas in search of food, thus propelling our species into a completely different environment and thus into a completely different economy.[29]

But in addition to the changing environment, the physical characteristics of our early primate ancestors were also very important factors. The possessing of a set of grasping hands and feet, opposable toes and thumbs, stereoscopic vision, and a bowed spine would all attribute to our ability to operate on two legs and ultimately free up their hands for other purposes, such as the making of weapons, shelters, and tools. Therefore without initially possessing these unique physical characteristics, we could have never survived outside the forests nor could we have evolved into the supreme nomadic hunters of world.[30]

And lastly, the inherent mental and social characteristics of our primate ancestors also played a huge role. By nature, they were aggressive, sexually vivacious, shrewd, curious, and somewhat organized, the very traits that would have thrust them onto new horizons. Hence, they were incredibly versatile creatures just waiting for the right circumstances to ignite their adaptation into another species. For better or for worse, they had already evolved into a creature that was totally prepared to forcibly ensure their survival by not only exploiting the other animals around them, but also those of their own species. While possessing the unique qualities needed to change their economy, they were prepared to move out onto richer environments and consciously alter their way of life. Undoubtedly, this was an unbeatable and deadly combination for a determined species on the move.

Chapter Two
The Food Gatherers
"Pre-australopithecines"

"The pre-human creature from which man evolved was unlike any other living thing in its malicious viciousness toward its own kind. Humanization was not a leap forward, but a groping toward survival."

Eric Hoffer (1902-1983)
American Author and Philosopher

Within the dense emerald forests of eastern Africa, our early pre-australopithecine ancestors were very much akin to the bonobo and common chimpanzees in their physical stature, mating practices, and social structure. And yet, there must have been several significant differences between us or our species would have remained in the vast forests. In all probability, our ancestors possessed a fiercer aggressive nature, a stricter patriarchal hierarchy, and a keener intelligence, which enabled them to seek out an alternative way of life as their forests began to disappear. In a very real sense, the small variations between our genetic codes would signify the difference between us remaining as food gathering apes (genus Pan) or eventually becoming nomadic humans (genus Homo).[1]

While always on the move looking for readily accessible food and water, our primate ancestors' way of life dictated no less as they were trapped within a world based upon what Mother Nature could provide them. Surrounded by prowling predators with very little sunlight penetrating the deep layers of vegetation, they would form their own unique roaming communities, or rather groups, so as to protect their territories. Comprising anywhere from 20 to 100 individual apes, these groups had developed a rigid social hierarchy that was maintained by their need to survive. However as a species, they were extremely successful, so long as the forests continued to expand.[2]

Spending the majority of their time among the towering trees, they were partially bipedal (walking upright) creatures. When they did move around on the ground, it was always in a crouching manner, using their hands and feet for propulsion (knuckle-walking). Standing over 4 feet tall and weighing close to 110 pounds, they were extremely agile creatures for their size, whose arms were longer than their undeveloped legs. While possessing the average size brain of well-over 400cc, they had an hour-glass shaped-head, a brow ridge, a large set of circular-shaped ears, a protruding wide jaw, and a pair of feet that were almost as nimble as their hands, which gave them the ability to glide through the tallest trees with the greatest of ease. Covered with a thick coat of dark wiry hair, their elongated shaped bodies were supported by a pair of bowed legs and knobby knees. And much like many other primates, they were born either left-handed or right-handed, depending upon which side of their brain controlled their motor skills.[3]

Our pre-australopithecine ancestors didn't possess the higher cognitive skills of modern humans. But much like the present day chimpanzees, they still displayed a surprisingly rich and diverse mental capacity. In addition to the ability to remember and classify objects according to their properties (e.g. size, color, smell, and shape), they could also recall and learn from their past experiences by reacting to a similar situation in a completely different fashion.[4]

For instance, they could actually come up with a totally different plan or strategy for overcoming a particular problem such as climbing a tall brittle tree, breaking open a thick nut, or hunting a prey. But most astonishingly of all, the children not only played with toys, but they also devised and then played different types of children games similar to tag or hide and seek. This incredible aptitude for remembering earlier events and images, classifying data, planning strategies, creating activities, and learning from their past mistakes was indicative of their ability to solve problems.[5]

Without question, this fundamental problem solving ability was directly related to the growing use of their hands and legs. As a way to adapt to their changing environment, our primate ancestors were unintentionally moving towards another economy. Along with their increased consumption of animal protein, which helped nourished the brain; their unique set of physical abilities had over time helped them develop their complex reasoning skills. In effect, the more animal protein they consumed, the more they were incline to use their arms and legs to obtain that protein. Ultimately, all of the necessary mental, physical, and dietary ingredients for eventually learning how to synthesize and analyze information were present within them. Therefore, it was just a matter of time before their descendants would begin to utilize a logical and sequential approach to any particular problem. However being highly emotional and credulous creatures, sometimes those emotions would interfere with their ability to clearly reason.[6]

It should also be noted that our pre-australopithecine ancestors in all likelihood possessed many of the altruistic qualities displayed by today's modern humans. As loving parents and companions, they exhibited a whole array of behaviors that aren't all that rare within the animal kingdom. On a daily basis, individuals could be observed caring for the sick and the injured, displaying stalwart loyalty to others, and mourning their dead. And just like many humans, some of them would forgo their immediate needs to assist others, protect and comfort the weak, or demonstrate the highest quality of all, the sacrificing of their own lives for the sake of their families and companions.[7]

As emotional and inquisitive creatures, they could display the capacity of expressing an astonishing range of joy or sadness, confidence or uncertainty, loathing or affection, bravery or cowardliness, and deceit or openness. Moreover, they were capable of crying whenever they grieved, grinning whenever they played, and yawning whenever they got bored. Yet, their incredible range of behaviors didn't stop there. As a member of a group and defined by that group, the individual ape's behavior was constantly being judged by the others around them. His or her reliability or untrustworthiness, selflessness or generosity, apathy or curiosity, timidity or assertiveness, and finally their forgivingness or resentment was all character traits noticed and remembered by the other apes. As a matter of fact, it was the frequency and the depth of these individual behavioral traits that helped define their personal identity and social status within the group. Although, our distant primate relatives could be quite brutal and violent, they were also emotionally vibrant, consciously devoted, and mentally resilient.[8]

There was one particular characteristic our pre-australopithecine ancestors doubtlessly exhibited that was handed down to us, which actually does separate us from the rest of the animal kingdom. Today's philosophers and historians have occasionally written about it, but only as an afterthought. In terms of our sheer survival, it is the most admirable and instinctual trait that we possess as a species. In essence, we are always at our best as a group, when things are at their worst. Whenever we find our group in dire straits, the very noble qualities of self-sacrifice, unselfish cooperation, and the total commitment to others have become the most prevalent traits within our species.

Then on a much darker side, our distant relatives were not only meat-eaters, but they also revealed a tendency towards cannibalism. They probably didn't start out as consumers of their own flesh. With the slow decline in the size of the enormous forests, they along with the chimpanzees were almost certainly forced to consume any available nutrition during the times of intense hardship. Survival was tough and without question it was rewarded to those who were prepared to change their eating habits.[9]

But whatever the circumstances, it wasn't beyond a male or a female to suddenly attack a small child of their own group and consume it right there on the spot, while the poor mother watched in horror. This type of unimaginable ruthlessness isn't an oddity within the animal kingdom. Many other mammals like bears, lions, pigs, otters, and opossums will also devour their young, along with many types of birds, insects, and fish. Nonetheless, if one considers the cold, stark reality of survival, it shouldn't be surprising to anyone that many carnivorous species can't distinguish the difference between eating the flesh of their own species or that of another animal. Within their highly competitive environment, a meal would be considered just another meal.[10]

In terms of our physical evolution, our primate ancestors had already developed a bowed spine, bent knees, collarbones, and a set of grasping hands and feet. In time, their later nomadic descendants would develop a broad pelvis bone, locking knee joints, elongated heel bones, and a lengthened set of big toes. Some of these characteristics evolved as a consequence of them living in the trees, while the others would come about as a result from them living on the ground. Thus, one of the main differences between our ancestral apes and the other apes in the forest was that our hominid ancestors began to progressively move towards the ground and eventually learned to thrive there with the other animals. This simple shift towards living on the ground had a profound impact upon our evolution. For it not only helped us to become more erect in our posture, while freeing up our hands for other uses, but it also assisted us in becoming more carnivorous in our feeding habits.[11]

As diurnal (daytime) creatures, they spent approximately 30 per cent of the daylight hours on the ground. Under normal circumstances, the males were expected to protect the group at all times, since they were physically bigger and stronger (sexual dimorphism) than their female counterparts. This sexual dimorphism possibly arose as a consequence of our species' sexual selection process, which resulted in the bigger and stronger alpha males' monopolizing a group's mating practices, and thus passing on their dominant genetic traits to their offspring.[12]

By and large, the forest's interlocking trees were a convenient refuge for them. Whenever they felt threatened or unsure of the situation, they could always scurry up a tree within a matter of seconds. Yet, it was the ground that provided them with the greatest opportunity to flourish. It was not only a place where they could find the most nutritious meals, but it was also a place where they could mate and satisfy their thirst for water. Unfortunately though, it was also a place of immense danger and death. Deadly predators lurked behind almost every tree just waiting for an opportunity to catch one of them out in the open. Thus in order to survive and function on the ground effectively, they had to begin to widen their communication and organizational skills at a very early stage of their development, so as to become a cohesive group.[13]

As territorial creatures, the primary group established their own particular territory within a certain geographic location. They would continuously mark it as a private possession with the scent of their urine and feces droppings. Sometimes this territory could cover up to 20 square miles, depending upon the size of the group. On occasion, their groups could roam up to 10 miles in search for food. Not too surprisingly, they could identify almost every plant within the forest by its sight, taste, or smell. As the forests most aggressive omnivores, they even knew what type of food was available and where it could be found during a particular part of the season.[14]

During feeding time, it was common for the primary group to break up into smaller bands that were composed of anywhere from 5 to 10 individual apes. Generally speaking, their daily movements were very leisurely and short in range. They spent their days either lazily grooming each other, mating, or inspecting and tasting the surrounding plant life. However once a desirable food came into season, they would gorge themselves as if it was their last meal. This feeding frenzy could last for days on end, because the best tasting foods were hardly available on a year round basis.[15]

As accomplished food gatherers, their eating habits were based upon what the different seasons of the year had to offer them. Hence many of their annual movements through the thick forest were inspired by their desire to reach a particular food before it was out of season. While moving from area to area, their consumption of bark, leaves, roots, berries, stems, and insects was just a temporary substitute, until the more desirable foods became available. In spite of the fact that they were always on the alert for unwanted intruders, they were able to leisurely eat a wide variety of different foods, which included an assortment of nuts, leaves, flowers, berries, fruits, bird's eggs, insects, and even honey. However, they were always on the lookout for fresh meat.[16]

Besides gathering their food from the surrounding trees, our pre-australopithecine ancestors did hunt down and kill an assortment of different animals for their meals. Sometimes this occurred during the dry season, when the plant food was scarce. But usually, it was a year round endeavor. Of course, they certainly weren't capable of hunting the much larger game that had wandered into the forests, but they were able to kill and eat a variety of baboons, wild hogs, bush pigs, bush bucks, young antelopes, and monkeys. [17]

As a rule, their tactics varied, depending upon the type of prey they were hunting. Individually, they were able to kill the infants of many different species so long as he or she could separate them from their mother. These encounters were almost always random in occurrence and within their own territory. But while hunting the larger and stronger adult prey, cooperation between the hunters was essential to their success. Using an assortment of different tactics, our primate ancestors were very effective in overcoming their intended victims. On occasion, a group of 10 or more males and sometimes a few females would go on a hunting binge lasting longer than a week.[18]

It would be a huge mistake to believe that our primate ancestors were a disorganized group of hunters, who randomly went through to the forest looking for their prey. In fact, they probably exhibited an extraordinary amount of teamwork, when it came to hunting. And how they were able to accomplish this amount of teamwork is not really known. But once they spotted a group of monkey in the trees, one of the hunters (driver) would climb up a tree and drive the monkeys towards a certain direction. Meanwhile, the rest of the hunters would run ahead in that direction so as to setup an ambush. As the main group of monkeys moved through the forest, several of the individual hunters (blockers) would split-off and create a wall along their pathway in order to funnel them towards the ambushers. Then once the monkeys had been forced into the ambushers, the blockers would arrive on the scene and capture the unlucky ones that weren't able to escape their trap.[19]

During the actual kill, our ancestors employed several brutal and frightening methods to overcome their prey. Since the prey's brain was usually the first part of the animal to be eaten, it was quite common for them to bite directly into the prey's neck or head for the quick kill. Sometimes, they flailed the body against a tree or the ground in order to stun it. Then on occasion, they just disemboweled the animal, tearing apart its flesh until the animal died. But whatever the bloody scenario, the hunters would then begin to scream, bark, or bellow out pant-hoots so as to alert the rest of the band of their good fortune. The competition for the precious meat was so fierce that it was quite common for them to display threats and even attack each other over their prize. If an adolescent or a low-ranking member of the band happened to make the kill, it was most likely that he or she would lose possession of the carcass to the more mature and higher ranking adults.[20]

Until we began to form family units, the distribution of the meat was accomplished through our ancestors' gender system. Since the males made most of the kills, it was their responsibility to distribute the precious meat as they saw fit. After the prey had been killed, they would gather around it and tear off large pieces of the viscera or an entire limb. Then as they individually moved off to one side, a parade of females and the younger males would begin to beg them for a piece of meat. If the beggar was a male ally or female love interest, they stood a much better chance of being fed. Needless to say, this system of food distribution wasn't very efficient, because only the stronger males and their allies were able to obtain a constant source of protein.[21]

These pre-australopithecine ancestors weren't actually the makers of tools. They didn't employ a hand-made tool to construct another type of tool (e.g. spears, axes, knifes, etc.). But in the beginning, they did use the surrounding branches, leaves, sticks, and rocks to their own benefit. With the development of their hands and minds, they were able to actually seek out other sources of food that many other animals weren't able to acquire. Accordingly, they could be called the users of nature's tools.[22]

As they searched for food among the thick forests, it was quite common for them to strip the leaves from a small twig and use it to catch insects. This was accomplished by poking a bare twig into the hole of an ant or a termite mound, until the insects had become sufficiently aroused. Aggravated by the intrusion, the insects would then begin to crawl up the twig into the ape's possession. In the meanwhile, they soon discovered that by using a stick to dig into the ground, they could easily obtain the many different types of tasty larvae, worms, and insects. It wasn't a hardy meal by any means, but it did provide them with a way of supplementing their diets.[23]

Besides trapping and digging for insects, they also used a variety of leaves and branches to construct their own temporary nests or beds. Usually, these beds could be found high in the trees, supported by the sturdy branches. Due to the height of the trees, these beds weren't just haphazardly thrown together. Instead, they were constructed in such a fashion as to ensure that the apes didn't fall through them or roll off the edges during a sleep-filled night. Undoubtedly, the construction of these temporary havens was well thought out beforehand, which was indicative of their growing intelligence.[24]

But the most important and intriguing skill that they possessed was their ability to break open fruits and nuts by beating them with a rock or a piece of wood. Oddly enough, it was this simple skill that would enable our early ancestors to change their economy and eventually revolutionize our species' evolution. Because once they had learned to use a hand-held rock to obtain food from the surrounding plants, it not only ignited their imaginations on the possibilities of using it for other purposes, but it also gave them the means to become scavengers.[25]

Employed as our first known hand-held tool, the rock also became our first and most reliable weapon. Of course, once we had become nomads, the simple rock would eventually evolve into the sharpened axe, long handled spear, or a sharpened cleaver. But in the beginning, our ancestors employed them as hand-held missiles. And without the use of weapons, we could have never successfully survived on the African savannas.[26]

These pre-australopithecine apes didn't establish an actual government per se, but their bands were organized into pecking orders. Within each of them, a dominant alpha male ruled over the other apes with the assistance of several beta lieutenants. He wasn't a supreme ruler in the sense of an absolute dictator, but he usually had his own way whenever he so desired it. Since primates emotionally express themselves through their actions and sounds, he communicated with his band in many different ways. At any given moment, he could employ a series of barks, pant grunts, yelps, pant hoots, and shrieks in order to express his disposition. Also hand gestures, body movements and postures, and facial expressions were used as a way of getting his message across. But whatever the method of communication, the dominant male ruled in accordance with his distinctive personality and his ability to manipulate others by constantly displaying his self-confidence, initiative, and his persistence.[27]

As the leader of a raggedy band of followers, his position of authority could be challenged at any time by the other male apes. Similar to the chimpanzees, these challenges were carried out between two individuals in a series of physical confrontations. Under normal circumstances, the younger male that could physically dominate the aging alpha male either through his acts of intimidation (displays) or by physically defeating him in a confrontation would be acknowledged by the others as the leader. On occasion, these conflicts could produce physical harm to one or both of the combatants.

And yet once a new leader had emerged, he usually led the band for about 10 years, before eventually being ousted by a much younger and stronger ape. Ranging in age from 20 to 26 years old, the alpha male commanded the trust and respect of the band's females. It was from his status as the major procreator and protector of the band's females that he could project his authority over the others. Thus, it was only after many years of maturing were the more assertive apes expected to step forward and fulfill a leadership role.[28]

The band's overall authority structure was based upon an individual's gender grouping. It was a system where the alpha male did not always dominate the other males by virtue of his greater strength and size, but sometimes by his ability to form allies with those around him. As for the females, they also had their own dominant individual. Similar to the males, this dominant alpha female was usually an older, larger, and more experienced ape. She primarily received her special status by the large number of offspring she had successfully produced and by her overriding temperament. Normally, she could dominate everyone within the band except for the mature males. Yet within her peer group and to the younger beta apes, she was the master of her own surroundings. Unfortunately, the omega females who happened to be barren and small in stature could expect a life of very little attention and even less recognition by the other apes.[29]

To say that we evolved from one of the most sensuous and sexually inclined creatures on this planet would be a profound understatement. Similar to today's humans, our primate ancestors participated in many different types of foreplay and physical intimacy before they actually had intercourse. Tongue touching, kissing, hugging, tickling, teasing, and even the oral fondling of each other were widespread behaviors that heightened the moment and strengthened their mutual pleasure. In fact, our ancestors' sexual relationships were an extremely important and time-consuming aspect of their lives.[30]

With the exception of the Bonobo apes and the dolphins, our primate ancestors were the only species that copulated all year round for reasons other than procreation. Possessed with the largest genitalia in the primate family, the males were constantly displaying a variety of courtship signals to the respective females as a way to reveal their sexual arousal. While experiencing an erection, they could attract the females either by their direct gaze, shaking a branch, hitting the ground with their knuckles, or by rocking themselves side to side. Sometimes, a female would respond to his signals and sometimes she wouldn't, thus leaving the male to look elsewhere for his satisfaction. While some male aggression and intimidation did take place, mature females often had a choice in sexual partners usually after a period of courtship. However, since they were promiscuous in their sexual relationships, a male could usually find a younger and less desirable female as a partner.[31]

Much like the chimpanzee's social structure, our primate ancestors functioned as a patriarchal society. Although, the females usually controlled the option to have intercourse with their desired mate, the males could still dominate them by their greater size and strength. As individuals, the males weren't allowed to spread their seed within another band for fear of being attacked and possibly killed by its jealous rival members. However, the females were free to go from band to band in order to procreate. In this manner, the group would always remain genetically flexible in spite of the males' restrictive movements.[32]

And yet, this does not mean that the deplorable acts of incest, pedophilia, or rape were unknown among our primate ancestors. Due to the male dominated social structure, these acts of violence would occasionally occur in order to satisfy the males' instinctual sex drive (libido) and to enhance his standing among his peers. This powerful sexual drive by the males possibly occurred for the same reason we became a dimorphic species. The bigger, stronger, and more sexually prolific alpha males monopolized the group's mating polygamous practices, and thus passed on their dominant genetic traits to their male offspring. Unfortunately to this very day, a female can find herself confronted by an overly aggressive unwanted suitor.[33]

Once the females reached the ages 10 to 11 and were ready to reproduce, they could expect to be mounted from behind by more than two consecutive males at a time. In this manner, it would ensure their pregnancy and the continuation of their species. Appearing as an unrestrained orgy at times, the beta males would literally ravage the females that the alpha males hadn't claimed as their own. The sexual excitement must have been almost unbearable for them. When the males weren't copulating, they were usually masturbating while awaiting their turn. On occasion in moments of extreme frustration, the males and females would look to their own gender for immediate satisfaction and acceptance. Many of today's scientists believe that they weren't really homosexuals in the modern sense of the word. But then on the other hand, some of our primate ancestors may very well have been homosexuals, considering their sexually hyper-active inclinations.[34]

This type of sexually hyper-active behavior was consistent with our predecessors' biological need to reproduce in great numbers. Moreover, it was one of the reasons why they were able to survive and eventually evolve into Homo sapiens sapiens. Coinciding with a females' heighten estrus period, the males' intense sexual desire (libido) to regularly reproduce was imperative for enlarging and maintaining their territory, so that they could successfully compete with the other primates. The extinction of any group of primates within the great forests would have occurred to those species that were incapable of occupying an area with a substantial number of their offspring. Competition was harsh and the most bountiful territories were actually battlefields between those in contention.[35]

Able to move freely from band to band, the mature females attracted the males with their unique scents and body movements. While coming into heat every 4 to 6 weeks, they were fertile for a period of 7 days. Due to the band's hyper-sexual inclination, the females could expect to be continuously pregnant, until they reached the age of 40. Similar to the rest of the females in the animal kingdom, they bore the burden of giving life. But once a female did become impregnated, the other female apes would shield her from the surrounding dangers until the moment of delivery. At that moment, she would move into the nearby bushes for protection and give birth to her child.[36]

After successfully conceiving a child, a female usually reared her children until they reached the ages of 6 or 7. It was during this long period of child rearing that they formed the most intense and enduring hominid relationship. Cradled in the mother's arms and finding nourishment from her breast, the child would become irreversibly dependent upon her for the needed food, warmth, and protection. Until it was time for the child to venture out into the world, they were inseparable. Yet amazingly and unlike many other species, if something happened to the mother and the child became an orphan, the other females within the band would raise the child as their own.[37]

Contrary to popular belief, this deep relationship between the mother and her children isn't a pair-bonding relationship. Instead, it is a maternal relationship based upon their biological/emotional dependency upon each other. The actual forming of a pair-bonding relationship between an unrelated male and a female did not exist among our primate ancestors. Though, it would eventually emerge, once we had become true nomads and began to form our family units. But in the beginning, our sexual relationships were basically a fission-fusion arrangement, or rather a cenogamy, where the individual females were free to breed with the other available mates within the groups. The children didn't really know or even care which male had actually fathered them. As long as the mother was present, they were assured a place of warmth and security.[38]

Undeniably, the relationship between a mother and her child is the most powerful relationship that exists between human beings. Biologically inspired and emotionally maintained, a mother and her offspring will find themselves eternally tied to each other. As a result, their relationship is so unique and everlasting for the child that many of today's psychological theories of behavior are based upon its internal dynamics. Modern children may love and respect their fathers, but under normal circumstances, they will almost always hold a binding devotion and a special place in their hearts for their mothers.[39]

As well as their individual identities, each group of apes possessed their own unique way of life. Some modern scientists have called it their cultural traits, while many others refer to it as their unique customs. But whatever the description, there were several subtle differences between the groups in how they lived, reacted in similar circumstances, and how they basically operated as a group. Their choice of foods, their preferred methods of communication, their approach to undertaking certain tasks, and even the way they used tools were all examples of their group differences. Not unlike the wide variety of human cultures that can be viewed today, the different groups of our ancestral apes were able to establish and maintain their own unique subcultures through the efforts of teaching the children their own way of life.[40]

For the offspring, their education started as soon as they left their mother's womb. The maze of jungle plants, wonderful colors, unusual sounds, and unforgettable aromas would come alive and become imprinted upon their very consciousness. Before long, they would be able to distinguish between the distinctively different characteristics of sights, sounds, and odors. By observing and then mimicking the other apes around them, the adolescents would begin to imitate the different calls, gestures, postures, and most importantly their behaviors. Comparable to all other hominids, the older apes acted as invaluable mentors, or rather as role models to the younger ones in passing along their important knowledge.[41]

While assimilating the different visual and auditory sensations from their daily encounters, the child's physical and social environments would soon become familiar landmarks as they began to learn how to communicate with their mother. Along with successfully expressing their own needs, these youngsters were quite capable of recognizing their mothers' moods, signals, routines, and different calls. Thus, it didn't take long before they became accustomed to the limits of their behaviors. While participating in the customary activities with the other apes, they were constantly learning which behaviors were permissible and which ones were not. Naturally, the rewards and punishments handed out to them by the adults were a significant part of their everyday lives.[42]

As they slowly ventured farther and farther away from their mother's protection, they learned how to recognize and deal with the different circumstances through trial and error. In many situations, it wasn't out of the ordinary for them to learn from their initial failures and mistakes. The hazards of scaling a brittle tree, wandering away from the security of the band, or attempting to play with a dangerous animal were invaluable moments for acquiring essential information. Also, it was during their early years that they were taught the many different needed skills for survival. Whether it was learning to climb a tree, wrestling with their peers, or playing chase, they were all important skills that would one day help them to survive the dangers of the forests.[43]

Amid the abundant plant life, our primate ancestors did more than just run away from their predators, procreate, or care for their young. Due to their superior intelligence, they undoubtedly came to rely upon the other animals around them for their survival, much like the later-day nomads. After concluding a feeding frenzy of either fresh fruit or meat, several types of smaller animals such as birds, squirrels, bush pigs, hares, foxes, jackals, and wild cats would begin to feed upon the left-over scraps. Forming a mutual symbiotic relationship, these animals not only became dependent upon those scraps of food, but they also benefited from the security provided by the band itself. Within the dark confines of the forest, they routinely followed the band from area to area in much the same manner as our domesticated pets follow us around the house. As a consequence, our ancestors quickly became aware of the many benefits of living alongside the other creatures of the world.

Living in a state of constant danger, these smaller animals exhibited certain behaviors or emitted various sounds as a form of communication. Used as an early warning system, our primate ancestors learned to make it a habit to listen and to watch them for any signs of unusual sounds or behavior. Employing a series of barks, chirps, screams, shrills, howls, or becoming overly restless in their movements, these companions of the forests would alert the band of any approaching dangers, such as predators, forest fires, or overflowing rivers. What's more, our ancestors soon discovered that by observing the animals, a lot of them could be used as a form of direction finder in locating water or certain types of plants. What the band didn't know about a particular area, the other animals could help them discover it. In fact, some creatures became so accustomed to our individual ancestors that they would actually lie down among them and clean the parasites off of their bodies, thus forming an inseparable mutual bond of companionship.

While our ancestral apes were still living in the tropical rain forests of eastern Africa, they probably initiated the close relationships that we enjoy today with our domesticated pets. Other animals have formed mutually supporting bonds between each other, but not nearly as profoundly as we have bonded with them. The reasons for this are quite simple. We learned very early in our evolution that animals can be feared, hated, ignored, or even eaten --- but that they can also be life savers, good companions, and very beneficial to our welfare. Due to this special bond between our earlier ancestors and the other animals in the forests, it is by no mere coincidence that as later-day nomads we were able to emulate the individual hunting skills of the cheetah or the coordinated attacks of the jackals, lions, and the hyenas. At that point, it had already become second nature with us to observe them and employ their talents.

As territorial and aggressive creatures, it was very common for our early ancestors to invade and then occupy another group's territory. Nor was it unusual for them to actively defend their part of the forest by continuously conducting patrols. Sometimes, this situation would lead to an agreed buffer zone between the two communities, much like a modern day demilitarized zone. Of course, this unwanted intrusion into another's territory wasn't accomplished peacefully. Due to social pressures brought about by either their diminishing food supply or by their overpopulation, a band of males, along with the more aggressive and larger females, would enter another group's territory in attempt to alleviate their hunger by sieging new territory. But instead of directly attacking another band of apes in one big confrontation, the invaders would attempt to individually ambush the male apes in the hopes of slowly killing off their alpha or beta males, thus intimidating the leaderless group to leave their territory. During these patrols, they occasionally encountered another band of apes of equal number, which would force them to make a hasty retreat. But once they ran into a lone ape, the invaders would begin to scream and violently shake the surrounding bushes; so as to momentarily stun their victim with fright and confusion. Then, they would finally pounced upon it with such force that the victim was usually torn apart and then eaten within a matter of minutes.[44]

This ruthless aggressive act of territorial expansion occurred on a regular basis, until the invaders had systematic killed off the adult males or at least forced the disheartened band to move to another territory. Afterwards, the victors would move their main group from their old territory into the new one, and enjoy the fruits of their aggression. Many of today's scientists and scholars believe that this period is when the human race propensity towards warfare first showed its ugly head. And there isn't any doubt that this supposition is beyond debate. Thus, it isn't surprising that our later-day nomadic, agrarian, and industrial societies have also exhibited the same inclination towards conquering their neighbors' territory over any number of political, religious, racial, geographical, and economic reasons.[45]

Nonetheless, it must be remembered that this early type of warfare was based upon our ancestors' economic imperatives, instead of their genetic makeup or their social norms. We aren't the only creatures on earth that will forcibly invade our own species' territory in an effort to occupy a richer area. Species of fish, birds, insects, and other mammals will also attack their neighbors, all in the name of territorial and economic necessity. Throughout time, the act of war by a species has always been a distinctive alternative to starvation and the possibility of extinction, which has made it almost instinctual in regards to our own behavior.[46]

As an economy, food gathering was very limited in its scope and depth. Yet, it was an economy that would eventually help physically and socially mode our ancestors into the species we are today. While developing the use of their arms and legs, along with increasing their consumption of animal protein, our ancestral apes would begin to further develop their physical and mental capabilities to the point where they were already beginning to dominate the forests. It was during this early period that they also began to slowly change from a semi-organized tree creature to a highly organized ground creature. Those physical and social changes were able to come about because of how they had initially developed among the deep forests of eastern Africa. In a very real sense, we can look upon the towering trees around us as not only our first shelters, but also as the birthplace of our species.

Amazingly, food gathering remains to this day a viable economy in some of the most remote parts of the world. In fact, the people who live along the many isolated river systems of central Africa, Asia, and South America have always gathered food for a living. Moreover, the natives who inhabit the South Pacific Islands still continue to reap the rewards of nature's bounty. From generation to generation, food gatherers have fished the oceans, lakes, and rivers, hunted the small game, consumed insects, collected fruits, berries, nuts, and eggs and dug for roots to satisfy their daily nourishment. Besides being our first economy, it is also the only economy that hasn't changed significantly in the last several million years.

Chapter Three
The Scavengers
"Australopithecines & Homo habilis"

"Man's most human characteristic is not his ability to learn,
which he shares with many other species, but his ability to teach
and store what others have developed and taught him."

Margaret Mead (1901-1978)
American Cultural Anthropologist

At the beginning of the Pliocene Epoch, around 5.3 million years ago, the earth's climate began to experience yet another and more profound cooler and drier period. As a prelude to the coming of the "Great Pleistocene Ice Age," the plush green forests of equatorial eastern Africa would begin to wither away with a renewed vigor. Predictably as the forests became smaller, the competition for food between the numerous animals became extremely fierce. As the nuts, flowers, fruits, seeds, bark, roots, berries, stems, and leaves became less abundant; the number of animals began to dwindle by the disruption of their food chain.[1]

In response to the changing environment, the animals of the forests were faced with a difficult choice. Either, they could remain in their diminishing surroundings and face starvation, and possibly their own extinction, or they could move out onto the open savannas and look for greener forests. For those animals that possessed the physical ability to live on the ground and were prepared to alter their eating habits, their mode of existence would never be the same again. After taking that first giant step towards moving out onto the savannas, they unknowingly began to change their species' forthcoming evolution.[2]

It was during this period of upheaval that several groups of anthropoid apes began to breakup into smaller bands and venture out onto the savannas in search of food, water, and shelter. Now whether they were forced out of the forests by another group of apes or they instinctively saw the writing on the wall and moved out onto the savannas on their own volition is not entirely known. In all probability, they were evicted from their territories by a more powerful group of apes. But whatever the circumstances, several bands of determined apes would eventually move out into a strange new world: a world of endless grass, blistering heat, circling vultures, and prowling predators of every shape and size. Undaunted by the task before them, they held true to their aggressive nature and valiantly risked their existence and those of their precious offspring. Unlike the present-day prosimians, which have physically remained the same for the last 60 million years, one particular species of anthropoid apes would one day evolve into the first human beings or into an Adam and Eve of sorts.[3]

Once the forests had begun to recede into a sea of grasslands, they left behind in their wake a number of flora covered areas along the meandering riverbeds and within the deep ravines, arroyos, and rugged canyons. Overflowing with a wide variety of trees and vegetation, these lowland areas were natural collection points of water from the rainwater that had fallen upon the eastern mountain slopes of the African Rift Valley. Providing a constant source of moisture for the plants and animals, these lowlands would become sanctuaries for the many types of animals, seeking relief and shelter from the sweltering sun and the surrounding dangers.[4]

Unable to live amid the vast savannas, our primate ancestors initially began to inhabit these small sanctuaries as a way of surviving. It was these isolated sanctuaries, or rather the remnants of the receding forests that would provide them with an area in which they could find food, water, and protection among the trees and undergrowth. As a result, these woodland islands would become havens for the many different types of australopithecines, such as the Australopithecus anamensis, A. afarensis, A. bahrelghazali, A. garhi, A. africancus, and the A. sediba, along with their Kenyanthropus and Paranthropus cousins, the P. aethiopicus, P. bolsei, and the P. robustus species.[5]

While in the process of moving from sanctuary to sanctuary in the hopes of finding food, shelter, and safety, they weren't accustomed to living among the tall grasses of the savannas, where the wind could blow for days on end and where there was very little food and even less protection. Thus, they almost exclusively dwelled in these rich sanctuaries as food gatherers, where they could build their dens, care for their young, and elude the larger predators. Not surprisingly, modern scientists have discovered the remains of our earliest primate ancestors within these same ancient ravines, caves, and deep canyons of eastern Africa, stretching all the way from southern Africa to Ethiopia, which is indicative of their movements out of the dwindling forests.[6]

The sudden appearance of the Australopithecus afarensis around 3.7 million years ago would signal the beginning of the human species as best as we can determine it. They were the first known hominids that didn't exclusively dwell in the forests. More ape-like than human in the shape of their skull, brain size (387-550cc), and in their facial features, the configuration of their pelvis and leg bones indicates that they were predominately bipedal creatures, which denotes that they could move erectly for some distance without having to use their arms for support. While being more graceful and slender (gracile) than the modern day apes, the average male stood around 5 feet tall and weighed less than a 100 pounds with the females being noticeably smaller. Even though they still looked like apes, their knee and pelvic bone structures, along with their smaller canine teeth were very human-like.[7]

Considering that the sanctuaries weren't that large in size and were quickly stripped of their food, the A. afarensis were forced to constantly move across the savannas from sanctuary to sanctuary in order to find another rich haven. And since they were barely able to depend themselves, it was essential that they avoided the surrounding predators. However, they did possess certain advantages. In addition to inheriting the social hierarchies, unique cultural traits, and the eating and mating habits from their tree-dwelling ancestors, they also inherited two distinctive skills that assisted them in surviving this new inhospitable environment.

First and foremost, the A. afarensis possessed the group skills needed for ambushing and then killing an unsuspecting prey. Passed on from generation to generation, this method of killing an animal by creating an organized ambush before they pounced upon it would have provided them with a significant source of protein. But due to their physical limitations, these early australopithecines didn't possess the physique or the organization skills to actually hunt down an animal on the savannas. Therefore, they were only able to employ this method of killing after an animal and its offspring had strayed into their sanctuaries. At that time, it must be remembered that these flora-filled havens had become the natural collectors of water due to their low elevation. Hence, it was not uncommon for a wide variety of thirsty animals to amble into one.[8]

Secondly, they also brought with them from the forests the ability to crack open the different types of nuts and fruits by using a simply hand-held rock or a wooden club. But unlike their primate forefathers and mothers, they also used the rock to crack open the bones of carcasses in order to obtain the nutritious marrow from the animals' bones that they had come across while moving from sanctuary to sanctuary. If this is the case and there is ample archaeological evidence that supports this notion, then over the span of time, the A. afarensis descendants would have learned how to use the rocks or clubs for other purposes, such as throwing them as a missile or using them as a hand-held weapon. Yet as food gatherers, they would continue to live much like their forbearers, eating mostly roots, berries, seeds, fruits, leaves, and insects that the sanctuaries provided them. Generally speaking, the A. afarensis might represent the link between our food gathering ancestors in the vast forests to the ones that eventually became scavengers.[9]

The transition of moving from the lofty trees to the ground must have been a long and painful one, but a significant one nonetheless. Even though these australopithecines still retained the agility to scurry up a tree in order to escape the larger predators, they had already begun forming dens and sleeping on the hard ground. Since the night was full of danger and the sanctuaries only had a limited number of trees and bushes, their small bands would begin to cuddle together around the alpha males. As in case of an approaching predator, the females were always in position to protect their offspring, while the males were free to deal with the predator as a screaming unified group. This type of new sleeping arrangement had not only afforded them a higher degree of security, but it also was the beginning of unconsciously forming a stricter patrilineal social organization.[10]

One of the main reasons the A. afarensis were able to survive the perilous dangers and hardships of trekking across the grass filled savannas was their eventual physical transformation towards becoming more erect in their posture. Obviously, this didn't happen overnight. It undoubtedly began the very moment that they were forced to leave the forests. While moving across the savannas from one sanctuary to another, it would have been almost impossible for them to have seen the approaching predators through the tall grass, until it was too late. Initially, they must have been forced to constantly stand up, so that they could peer over the tall grasses and observe a much wider area. Then later, they would begin to use their legs as a way of predominately crossing the savannas and eluding the predators. By slowly abandoning their knuckle-walking posture, they soon discovered that they could move much faster, quieter, and even farther by standing erect.[11]

And yet, there were also other advantages to becoming more erect that further induced our ancestors' physical adaptation. In addition to keeping themselves relatively cool by positioning their backs away from the unrelenting sun, they also began to slowly lose their hairy coats, which probably initiated the development of their sweat glands. This new found physical ability of shedding their internal heat by sweating would as a result lower the individual's heightened temperature by pulling the excess heat out of the body.

Although, our ancestors' ability to sweat created a superior cooling mechanism, as compared to the other animals, it also created a greater dependency upon their consumption of water, which they could have easily obtained within the sanctuaries' creek beds, various watering holes, or by eating the savanna's water-laden succulent plants. Nevertheless, as our primate ancestors became more erect and mobile, it also helped them to develop the ability to survive out in the open savannas by freeing up their hands to protect themselves from predators. As a consequence, their descendants (H. ergaster/erectus) would eventually be able to leave Africa and make the economic leap to one of nomadic hunting.[12]

For the A. afarensis, the African savannas were a whole new world filled excitement, wonder, and dread. They shielded their eyes from the bright noon day sun, struggled through the unfamiliar harsh winds, and drank from the muddy watering holes. Their feet, knees, and backs persistently ached from having to walk upright. They carried their children for long distances as they slowly travelled over the landscape, pausing only long enough to peer over the tall grasses. Always on the alert and always watchful, they were constantly sniffing the air for any scent of danger. They attempted to conceal their movements by wandering through the shallow arroyos and the dried river beds, knowing full well that their lives depended upon their elusiveness. And yet when they were discovered by a group of hungry predators, they died a hard and terrible death, where their screams could be heard echoing through the wind.

They were awkward and scrawny looking creatures, who were always living on the edge of survival. Caught between two dilemmas, they could either remain within their diminishing sanctuaries or they could venture out into the unknown savannas. Constantly facing the threat of starvation, they were forever being pulled into the wind-blown savannas in search of richer surroundings. Driven by the need to find food for their children, they would slowly move from one sanctuary to another, while constantly on the lookout for any discarded carcasses or roaming predators. Almost defenseless, their lives were filled with uneasiness and dread as they never wandered very far away from each other. Their continued survival demanded no less from a group of uneager and wandering newcomers. While slowly learning how to adapt to a strange and hostile environment, they must have been very desperate and fearful creatures, whose only chance of living another day was their ability to function as a unified group. It was only within these small faithful bands that they could have found the determination to overcome the dangers and uncertainties around them.

This gradual physical transformation from being a tree dwelling omnivorous creature to becoming a predominantly carnivorous nomadic hominid (H. ergaster/erectus) took approximately 3 million years to occur. It was during this lengthy time that many different types of early hominids were also struggling to survive in their diminishing and over-populated sanctuaries. Although, they were also fairly erect in their movements and able to function on the ground for long periods of time, some of these creatures like the Paranthropus and Kenyanthropus species weren't able to make the jump to living exclusively on the savannas where the vast herds of animals had roamed. In due course, they would disappear from the scene along with the A. afarensis.[13]

Many of today's scientists believe it was either the Australopithecus africanus or the A. garhi that was the evolutionary link between the earlier A. afarensis and the first known Homo species, the Homo habilis. Of course, there were some physical differences between them, which have produced a number of questions as to their actual place within the human family tree. Nonetheless many of their physical traits are consistent with today's evolutionary models that have been programmed to illustrate how we must have evolved. But whatever the archaeological arguments, it was one of the more recent australopithecines that began to make the economic transition to becoming a true scavenger.[14]

Appearing around 3.3 million years ago in eastern Africa, the A. africanus/garhi were not only the users of rocks, but quite possibly that of the long thick tree branches that they had found within the sanctuaries. Without question, these particular skills would have been essential for them to have made an attempt towards scavenging. Possessing a smaller brain (400-450cc) then the A. afarensis, but the same physical features, they didn't actually live on the savannas. But, they did rely upon them for their basic nutritional needs. And unlike their food gathering ancestors of the great forests, who had sat around and waited for an animal to stumble into their ambush, these particular australopithecines were undoubtedly forced to move out onto the savannas in order to scavenge whatever carcasses they might come across. This might have been due to the shrinking and the eventual disappearance of the sanctuaries, which led to the depletion of their food supply. Or quite possibly, they were forced out by the other australopithecines. But whatever the circumstances, our ancestors were going to have to find other sources of nourishment in order to survive.[15]

Initially, their forays must have been short in duration and not very far from their sanctuaries. As the older males quietly and desperately moved out into the arid savannas, they began finding and eating the scraps of the left-over carcasses that had been abandoned by the larger predators, such as leopards, bears, and lions. While avoiding the other animals around them, they would return to their sanctuary with the carcass. But as our ancestors continued to physically increase their erect-like mobility and become more proficient in their organizational and communication skills, these daring incursions would increase in both their duration and distance.

It should be pointed out that the modern day image of a docile A. africanus/garhi isn't an entirely accurate picture. As a semi-organized group of aspiring young scavengers, they were in all likelihood more skilled and formidable than previously thought. With the exception of confronting a den of large predators, they were very capable of defending themselves against the marauding packs of smaller predators. In all likelihood, the surrounding animals had become leery of them. This doesn't mean to imply that these australopithecines were actual hunters, because they certainly weren't. But, it does mean they must have possessed an effective weapon system that could have driven away the smaller predators from their freshly killed carcass.[16]

With the development and increased use of their hands and arms, the first hominid hand-held instrument must have been the ordinary rock. It was simple to use, conveniently available, and it didn't have to be produced. Initially, these rocks weren't used as tools as many modern scientists have theorized. In fact, they must have been used as crude weapons to be thrown at a threating predator. Only later would the rock be employed as a tool in order to chop-up the carcasses that they had acquired by the use of their new-found weapons.

Originally, the A. africanus/garhi attempted to conceal their movements, while they walked through the savannas looking for carcasses. Consisting of anywhere from 5 to 15 individuals, they slowly moved through the tall grass picking up the available rocks and looking up into the sky in search of vultures. These birds of prey were easy to spot even at a very long distance as they circled high above a freshly killed carcass. Although, this method was very time consuming, it was the safest tactic they could employ amid so many predators. However once they had gained a degree of confidence in their ability to protect themselves with their new found weapons, our ancestors would head straight for the circling vultures without any regard for being observed.[17]

Once our ancestors had come upon a pack of small predators and their carcass, they began to scream and yell at the top of their lungs as they bombarded them with a continuous barrage of rocks. Momentarily stunned by the noisy chaos, the predators would have unexpectedly found themselves in the position of either being stoned to death or seriously injured. Thus, our ancestors could have easily taken possession of the carcass once the pack of frightened predators had abandoned their meal. Over time, this simple tactic of creating chaotic scene by screaming and then by bombarding the predators with a hand full of rocks was so effective that our ancestors began to employ it against their own species and that of the other hominids in the form of territorial combat.[18]

It was this ability to kill or to maim at a distance that gave the A. africanus/garhi an edge that no other animal possessed. And undoubtedly, the use of rocks as weapons spread like wildfire throughout the other scattered bands. And yet, they must have realized fairly quickly that the only way to approach a pack of small predators, while they were feeding on a carcass, was by keeping their group together. In this manner, they were able to concentrate their barrage of rocks into a steady stream of missiles which would have driven the smaller predators away. However on occasion, a desperate pack of hungry predators would stand their ground and fight for their carcass. In which case, our ancestors would have made a hasty retreat in the hopes of eventually returning to the scene to look for the scraps. Of course, the simple rounded rock wasn't a very effective weapon for hunting. Even at a short distance, it would have been almost impossible for them to have killed a prey with a blunted rock. Yet, it would have been an enormously effective weapon in obtaining a carcass from a pack of small predators or in scaring off a larger predator.[19]

Unlike the other scavengers in Africa that consumed their preys' entire carcass right there on the spot, our ancestors would first eat the mineral rich entrails and then carry the rest of the carcass back to the sanctuary in order to feed the others in their band. This routine not only rewarded our more aggressive and daring ancestors with an opportunity to eat the tastiest and most nutritious parts of the carcass, but it also explains how the other australopithecines that had remained behind in the sanctuaries were able to eat.[20]

The utilization of weapons was very important to our ancestor's survival. Within a span of approximately 1.5 million years, our ancestors had evolved from living as food gatherers within the thick forests to one of becoming aggressive scavengers upon the savannas. In actuality, the use of rocks was the first time in our evolution that we began to assertively use the objects around us as weapons. For instance, it's one thing for a species to beat open a piece of fruit with a rock for its nourishment, but it's quite another to use that same rock as a weapon in order to overcome the other competing animals and thus propelling themselves up the food chain. In all likelihood, this was one of the main reasons why such a significant number of our ancestors were able to thrive among so many predators.[21]

Since the A. africanus/garhi weren't full-blown hunters, their consumption of meat entailed a small percentage of their overall diet. However once the sanctuaries began to diminish, their meat intake would rapidly increase as they ventured farther out into the savannas looking for carcasses. Undoubtedly, this new source of protein had given them the required energy and motivation to seek out even more carcasses. Hence, it is not unlikely that they developed a certain expertise within their various limited skills. Over time, they would have come to recognize the best methods in scaring away the hungry predators, along with which species were the easiest to panic. But whatever the circumstances, the surrounding rocks weren't the only tools that nature had provided them. They also brought with them from their ancestors early days, the knowledge of how to use a sturdy tree branch as a way of separating themselves from a dangerous predator.

In point of fact, a long tree branch probably became a very useful tool to the hungry scavengers. Comparable to a simple rock, it could have been employed as an effective device in order to keep the other scavengers at a distance or even to scare them off. While creating a chaotic scene with their loud screaming, this could have been accomplished by either thrusting or waving a long forked-tip branch at any threatening animal. In this fashion, it wasn't actually used as a weapon, but rather as a way of keeping it away.[22]

Logically, the A. africanus/garhi must have learned from their ancestors that much of their survival was based upon keeping them a safe distance from danger. The act of throwing a rock or waving a long wooden branch at a vicious animal wouldn't have been a giant evolutionary step for them to have taken. In fact, they couldn't have survived as long as they did without adapting to some degree. As a result, it is by no mere coincidence that the simple rock and wooden branch would very quickly evolve into the hand-held axe and the common spear.

The social changes brought about by slowly moving towards a scavenging economy would have had a very profound effect upon them. In response to the increase of danger in directly competing with other scavengers, the bands' unity and cooperation became paramount in a world of open spaces. Forced to venture farther out into the sunbaked savannas, the A. africanus/garhi suddenly found the need to better organize their bands. Times were harsh, food was scarce, and the only way they were going to survive was to change the way their leaders were selected.

Instead of the alpha males being determined by which of them could scream the loudest or jump the highest, the leadership roles of the bands were bestowed upon the ones that could bring back the most food and effectively protect the others against the marauding predators. As a consequence, the role of the alpha males and females, who had previously led their particular gender groups in the deep green forests, was actually expanded and intensified. Out of pure necessity, the leaders of each band were forced to increase their dominance over the others by exerting their authority on a more consistent basis. Obviously, this wasn't an easy task to accomplish. But if they were going to have any chance of surviving the savannas, the alpha males and females would have had to direct their bands in a more physical manner.

Moreover, the relationships between the members of the band were altered in a way that allowed the males to almost completely dominate the females. For the first time in our existence, the females would become almost exclusively dependent upon the males to provide them with their primary nourishment from the savannas. The days of individually gorging themselves on the bounty of the forests were long gone. As a prelude to the more recent nomadic economy, the males not only became primarily responsible for the females and their children's protection from the predators, but they also began to dominate the band's sexual practices. From this point on, the females weren't allowed to mate with a member from another band. As a matter of fact and unfortunately, the females wouldn't be able to completely free themselves from the males' economic, political, and sexual dominance, until our societies had become industrialized.[23]

It was during these early days of survival, when our primate ancestors were just beginning to succeed as scavengers, a behavioral pattern would begin to emerge in regards to how we perceive ourselves as a species. Living from hand to mouth, amid dangers that appeared to lurk behind every bush and tree, the different bands would come to look upon each other as the primary threat to their own existence. Certainly, the surrounding predators were dangerous creatures that would occasionally attack and even kill one of our primate ancestors. But, they didn't represent a serious threat to the existence of the whole band. The only species that possessed that ability were the other roaming bands of hominids. As direct and related competitors, our ancestors had the option to either drive another band away from their havens or to systematically kill off their most dominant males. In either scenario, it spelled certain doom to the unfortunate band that had become leaderless and stranded on the unpredictable savannas. This new form of personalized warfare between the scavenging bands would become uncommonly ruthless and unforgiving.[24]

When our primate ancestors lived in the thick green jungles and forests as food gatherers, they had always fought against each other as a way of gaining new territories. By successfully ambushing the individual males of a rival group, an aggressive group could eventually push them out of their territory. Yet as scavengers, their warfare would take on a whole new dimension in its animosity and brutality. For the first time, our warfare was based upon one band fighting another band, instead of one band ambushing a lone individual. But, it was also the first time that we would employ the use of weapons. On a fairly regular basis, these bands were forced to confront each other whenever they were scavenging for food on the grassy savannas or whenever they were attempting to push another band out of their sanctuaries. Usually, these confrontations started out as a form of boisterous demonstration with the outnumbered band eventually backing away. But if their numbers were about equal, the confrontation could end up becoming very violent.[25]

With the sudden appearance of an adversary, the alerted bands would cautiously move towards each other in a crouching manner. Much like approaching a predator and its carcass, the individuals within each band began to bunch up into a tight formation with the alpha males in the forefront. Then, they would pause for a second and look around for an escape route in case they had to withdraw. As they moved closer to each other, they began waving their arms in the air and screaming at the top of their lungs as a form of demonstration, which could last for several minutes. Then at a fight or flight distance of around 20 feet, they would suddenly stop and confront each other by fiercely growling and exposing their elongated fangs and hand-held rocks, thus creating a very intense standoff.

It was at this point, the more aggressive individuals began hurling their rocks at their nearest opponent. Within a matter of a few minutes, the engagement was usually decided upon by which band could produce the heaviest and most accurate barrages. It was a very primitive form of battle, but a battle nonetheless. Then once the losers had been forced from the field of contention, the winners would begin to celebrate their victory in the form exuberant bellows, dancing, and chest-pounding. Even though their main intention was to discourage and then scare away the other band, the casualties could be substantial in relationship to their small numbers.

Today, these rock-throwing contests may appear to be extremely primitive and harmless by our standards, but they could be very deadly affairs. One well-placed rock to the head or to the chest area could have permanently disabled or even killed an opponent. Needless to say, the bands with the largest number of males had a decided advantage over the smaller ones. They could literally overwhelm them by throwing a more intense barrage of rocks. However, the smaller bands had an excellent opportunity to overcome them, if they could initially kill or knock out of action their opponent's leader (alpha male). After finding themselves leaderless, the larger band would usually dissolve into a panic stricken mob of retreating individuals.

Since their bands occasionally operated in the same general vicinity and were able to identify each other by their various physical characteristics and body odors, the conflicts between them were extremely personal, vicious, and unyielding. Familiarity breeds contempt and contempt breeds fear, which leads to unbridled cruelty, especially among those creatures that are competing against each other for the same ecological niche.

In actuality, these bitter conflicts between the australopithecine bands must have had an everlasting effect upon our psyche. Quite early in our evolution, we began to demonstrate a malicious behavior towards our own species in the fight for survival. It was an economic struggle for territory and carcasses, compelled by our ancestors' need to eat and bear their offspring. The rules of engagement were very simple: there weren't any rules. The winners would live another day, while the losers might very well perish under the wind- swept African sun.

Thus, the deplorable human trend of man's inhumanity towards man, or rather the belief that "might makes right," began to appear quite early in our evolution. Not surprisingly, it is this preconceived notion of viewing the strongest and the most aggressive groups of our species as superior to the others that has fostered our less admirable traits on a local and international level. Wars, rebellions, genocides, atrocities, starvations, ethnic cleansings, and the mass removals of whole peoples are but a few historical examples of our instinctual inability to live as one.

In response to the unrelenting dwindling forests and the expanding savannas, the A. africanus/garhi continued to live amid the thick flora sanctuaries of the riverbeds, ravines, and canyons. Physically incapable of permanently living on the plains, their populations would remain in their sanctuaries, while scavenging the remains of carcasses and eluding the surrounding dangers on the savannas. However with the coming of the Great Pleistocene Ice Age, the earth's environment would begin to experience a succession of climatic changes, characterized by alternating periods of arid shivering cold to periods of warm muggy humidity. It was during one of these sudden environmental shifts, a new hominid species would suddenly appear in eastern Africa. Yet unlike their australopithecine cousins, these creatures were the first known species to be classified as the genus Homo (human).[26]

To this day, modern scientists aren't really certain whether we directly descended from the H. gautengensis, the H. habilis (handy human), or from the H. rudolfensis, emerging together around the same period approximately 2.5 million years ago. According to the current physiological models, they possessed many of the same physical characteristics, while also exhibiting a few others that could exclude them from our family tree. In spite of this, there is a very real possibility that they were all actually the same species or even a different species of the australopithecine family. As a result, some researchers believe they shouldn't even be classified within the Homo genus, as they were more apelike than human. They defiantly point to the H. ergaster as our first Homo genus. Nevertheless, it was one of these creatures or quite possibly another one which hasn't yet been discovered that was the economic link between the scavenging A. africanus/garhi and our more recent nomadic ancestors, the H. ergaster/erectus. And since the H. habilis has been recognized by the majority of the world's scientific community as a separate and identifiable species, they appear to be the best candidate for now.[27]

Multiplying in the numerous ravines, canyons, and river bottoms, the Homo habilis were about 5 feet tall and weighed just over 100 pounds.

With an elongated shaped body and a pair of undeveloped arms that hung almost down to their knees, they were definitely bipedal creatures, who must have been much more skillful and physically gifted than previously thought. One the most interesting aspects about them as compared to the earlier hominids was the increase in the size (590-687cc) and complexity of their brain. Small as compared to the size of a modern day human's brain, but still larger than that of the australopithecines, one of their discovered craniums reveals a visible bulge inside the Broca's area, which unmistakably indicates the aptitude for speech.[28]

Since we may never know for sure, it is fairly safe to assume that the development of human speech was a progressive phenomenon that possibly began with the tool-making H. habilis. As an evolving species, the individual barks, grunts, yelps, and shrieks that they verbalized would in time evolve into actual rudimentary words by our later-day ancestors. Based upon the unique sounds (phonetics) produced within each band, the vocalized forms of guttural and high-pitched pronunciations would have eventually become the basic structure of our ancestor's primitive words (morphology). Then much later in our evolution, a particular combination of syllables or words would have been accepted within each nomadic clan to have a specific meaning and eventually handed down to their children as the first spoken languages.[29]

Such things as an emotion, an object, an idea, a command, a behavior, or a location were all areas of the human experience that were ultimately labeled and then expressed in our ancestors' verbal exchanges. Within the course of everyday affairs, they would have also created a wide variety of sounds to identify the many different plants, animals, and tools. Moreover, they would have begun making specific sounds towards certain individuals in the form of names. It was through these simple forms of sounds that our later-day nomadic descendants were eventually able to form syntaxes, which assisted them in better organizing themselves for the purpose of hunting and competing with the other groups of hunters.[30]

The economic pressures to organize themselves better by expanding their communication skills must have been immense. The required leadership role needed to control and direct a band of scavenging primates could only have been achieved, and then sustained, through the development of their verbal and nonverbal language skills, such as sign and body languages. Commands had to be given by the leader and acknowledged by the followers, so as to ensure their success by functioning as a manageable group. In order for the H. habilis to have successfully organized any kind of scavenging excursions, teach their offspring and uphold their social hierarchy, they would have been literally forced just out of economic necessity to begin the long process of developing our ability to verbally communicate.

By beginning to learn how to express themselves to each other in recognizable forms of simple guttural sounds and body movements, it would have made the difference between life and death for any species attempting to find new sources of food in an unfamiliar environment. Of course, the development of our language skills has taken millions of years. But as it slowly occurred, its impact would have been steadily felt throughout the whole world. As it will be discussed later, there has always been a direct relationship between the remarkable development of our hands, weapon/tool making and language skills, and that of our increased mental capacity.[31]

The discovery of the H. habilis was a very important event in understanding and piecing together our development. Although, tool making could have occurred in a much earlier time by a different species, the H. habilis were the first recognized hominids to have constructed them. Referred to as the Oldowan stone industry, it is believed by today's scientists that these hand-shaped chipped rocks were made for the purpose of scraping, cutting, and chopping up the remains of large animals. However, they must have been initially used as weapons, since there wouldn't have been a need to construct a tool for cutting up a large carcass without first possessing the ability to obtain it.[32]

In all probability, the Oldowan flaked stones were used as both a weapon and a tool. For instance, some of the stones were chipped on one side and used as a slicing blade to scrape, cut, or chop meat. However, they also must have been used as an improved throwing stone. With the stone sharpened at one end, the projectile would have become deadlier in its impact upon a predator than by using a blunted rock.[33]

Furthermore, some of the stones were constructed like the head of a spear with a protruding point. Used as a tool, it would have been very effective in digging into the ground or in penetrating the tough flesh of a dead animal. But as a hand-held weapon, it could have been used to repel a direct attack by an aggressive predator. In fact, these two very different types of chipped stones in all likelihood enabled our ancestors to scavenge the larger carcasses, thus making the stones the very first weapon/tool that we actually made with our own hands.[34]

While possessing the required innate ruthlessness, social hierarchy, and hand-related skills needed to effectively overcome much of their competition, the H. habilis didn't have to confront the dangers around them as a helpless band of individuals. As a semi-organized group of rock-carrying individuals, they were able to function and survive within an unforgiving and hostile environment. With the aid of a hand-made weapons system, these awkward looking creatures must have been a formidable foe as compared to their tree-dwelling ancestors. In all likelihood, they were the first hominids that had developed enough organizational skills to actually kill the grazing animals out on the savannas. This could have been accomplished by chasing the already skittish herd into a muddy river bottom or over a steep cliff of a canyon. In either scenario, the H. habilis would have had an opportunity to easily overcome them without having to deal with the dangerous predators.[35]

Without a doubt, the act of hunting was a very significant step in our evolutionary and economic drive towards moving out into the vast savannas. Inspired by the need to find richer surroundings and to provide food for their young, they would slowly find themselves moving into another ecological niche by becoming more organized, carnivorous, and mobile.

The development of the Oldowan tool industry ensured our ancestors survival within their sanctuaries. But, it was also the beginning of our continuous technological revolution that is still taking place to this very day. Within the abundant shrubs and clumps of trees in eastern Africa, these awkward looking creatures would begin to venture farther and farther out onto the savannas with their hand-made implements to forge a new beginning. It was a beginning filled with danger and uncertainty, essentially inspired by the dwindling sanctuaries and their need for food. Whether or not they were noble, courageous, and admirable creatures is a matter of one's own perception about our own species in general. But there can be little doubt that our scavenging ancestors were determined, semi-organized, and very adaptable creatures.[36]

Over a period of time, the australopithecines and the H. habilis initiated and then laid the foundation for their descendants to become true nomads. By intentionally and permanently moving out of the forests and altering their diet towards a more bountiful way of life, they helped establish our future uniqueness. These unimposing apelike creatures would mark a significant milestone in our evolution by taking a defiant and giant step towards moving out onto the savannas and altering their economy towards scavenging. As a dynamic young species, they began to consciously overcome their surroundings by becoming more erect in their posture, while at the same time, constructing the first human hand-held weapons and tools. Meanwhile, they undeniably began the long drawn out process of learning how to communicate between each other in an effort to better organize their bands for scavenging. And by doing so, they would forever change the lives of their future generations.[37]

Chapter Four
The Lower Paleolithic Nomads
"Homo ergaster/erectus"

"Historians will have to face the fact that natural selection determined the evolution of cultures in the same manner as it did that of species."

Konrad Lorenz (1903-1989)
Austrian Zoologist and Ethologist

Ever since the Precambrian Period, the earth has intermittently experienced an Ice Age. At intervals of approximately every 150 million years, a major one will appear and wreak havoc across the globe. Presently, the world's geologists have determined that an Ice Age will last a few million years at a time. But no one really knows for sure how long they will truly last, or for that matter, why they come at all.

However, there are several theories as to why we have them. Many scientists have theorized that the earth's orbit around the sun will periodically fluctuate (Milankovitch cycles) from its regular rotation, thus altering its axis and diverting the sun's rays away from the poles. While many others believe that the shifting of the earth's continental plates has been the real instigator, thereby disrupting the direction of the hemispheric winds and the oceans' currents. And finally, a number of scientists have come to propose that the answer can be found in the changing of the earth's atmospheric composition, especially the concentration of greenhouse gases. But for whatever the reasons, there is little doubt that this present Ice Age has had a tremendous impact upon the development of our species.[1]

During a typical Ice Age, the earth will experience a succession of expanding and then receding polar glaciers, which occurs within three distinctive phases. Without question, each of these phases could be classified as a catastrophic event in and of itself. It is during the first phase that the earth's atmospheric temperature will steadily plummet as its polar ice caps become larger and larger. In general, the winters will become progressively longer and harsher as the world's oceans, rivers, and lakes begin to shrink with the absorption of water into the polar caps, thus eventually creating a succession of severe droughts.[2]

Then at the beginning of the second phase (glaciation period), the mounting pressure from the enlarged ice caps becomes so great that they will eventually form huge glaciers and begin to move, or rather expand away from the earth's poles. During this expansion process, which can last up to 100,000 years at a time, the glaciers will gradually bulldoze everything within their paths. Over an extended period of time, they will literally push a region's top-soil and lose rock formations, along with its indigenous plant and animal life into a totally different region. For instance, the towering pine and maple trees that presently cover the southern states of the North American continent were originally brought down from Canada. It has even been speculated by the world's geologists that some of these huge glaciers of shifting ice were capable of traveling several thousand miles and reaching up to 10,000 feet in height. Therefore once the process of glaciation has reached its apex, only a relative confined portion of the earth's land surface was actually inhabitable.[3]

Geologically, the impact of glaciation upon the earth's surface has been immense. Besides literally pushing the plant and animal life into a different region, the resulting friction created by the crushing rocks within these glaciers will form a fine dust called loess. Presently, this fine dust can be found all over the earth's surface. Furthermore, once the glaciers have finally receded back to their poles, they will leave behind in their paths a series of huge mounds and ridges (moraines), deep valleys (cirques), large bodies of water (tarns), and an assortment of scratches on the remaining rock formations (striae). Within the average Ice Age, the process of glaciation can occur many times over, depending upon how long it lasts.[4]

Along with the geological record, the existence of the third phase (interglacial period) can also be found in our oldest manuscripts and religious texts. It is a period of extensive global flooding and the eventual renewal of life itself. Lasting between 15,000 to 30,000 years at a time, the glaciers will begin to slowly melt and recede back to the poles from whence they came. The barren and uninhabitable lands will reappear from beneath their icy graves. With the rise in the earth's temperature, the water from the dissolving glaciers will literally flood much of the earth's land surface. The previously diminished oceans, lakes, and rivers will overflow, turning the arid flatlands into insect infested swamps. Over time, the flooding will eventually recede as the plants reemerge, thus inducing the animals to move slowly back northward in order to reclaim the land.[5]

Commencing about 2.5 million years ago, our planet began to experience its fifth major Ice Age, the "Great Pleistocene Ice Age." The continents were essentially in their present locations as the succession of glaciation periods covered at least 30% of the earth's land surface with some of the glaciers reaching the 40th parallel north of the equator. While disrupting the delicate eco-systems over large areas of North America, Europe, and Asia, the glaciers would alter the direction of the earth's major river systems, created thousands of lakes, widened the valleys, reshaped the mountains, and deepened the canyons. It was during this period that a number of deserts in Asia (Arabian and Gobi) and Africa (Sahara) began to further expand as a result of the decrease level of rainfall. Meanwhile, the ocean levels would rise and fall with the coming and the going of these glaciers, altering their currents and leaving behind a massive sheet of ice across Antarctica. With the alternating of the climate, our ancestors along with the northern herds of animals were either moving towards the equator in order to avoid the ice or migrating northward into their old hunting grounds, once the glaciers had receded. Overall, it was a time of tremendous climatic changes and global upheaval that would directly propel our species evolution.[6]

During this time, the Homo ergaster (working human) appeared and began to slowly migrate out of Africa and into the continent of Asia. A large number of today's scientists have concluded that our direct line of descent begins with the H. ergaster and that they eventually evolved into the Asian Homo erectus and then later into the European Neanderthals, thus leaving the Homo erectus (upright human) out in the cold. However many other scientists believe the H. erectus is a very important species in our evolution. They claim the African H. ergaster should be classified as a later version of the H. habilis, which eventually evolved into the H. erectus. They also assert that the species H. georgicus, H. pekinensis, and the H. heidelbergensis are really a subspecies of the H. erectus and not that of the H. ergaster. But whatever the consensus, if there ever is one, it doesn't really matter here. What we do know for sure is that they were definitely nomadic in their way of life.[7]

It was the H. ergaster/erectus species that started our evolution towards becoming considerably more "human." Possessing a larger brain (750-1250cc) than their predecessors, they began to cultivate many new skills, such as improving their weapon/tool industry, erecting temporary shelters, wearing crude clothing, and controlling the use of fire. But even more importantly, they were also able to change their economy from one of scavenging to nomadic hunting by demonstrating a significant improvement in their ability to hunt the larger game as a coordinated group. Therefore, it is no small wonder that they are considered a very important link to our economic evolution.[8]

As a major forerunner of modern humans, the mighty H. ergaster/erectus ultimately arose and came to dominate the continents of Africa and Eurasia. Incredibly, they existed for a tremendously long time. Emerging approximately 1.8 million years ago, they finally became extinct about 53,000 years ago or less. Without a doubt, they were much more advanced in their skills than previously thought. Besides existing for such a long period of time, they also left in their wake a considerable number of subspecies. As a nomadic creature, the H. ergaster/erectus had a unique economic method in dealing with any threat to their immediate survival. Whenever the competition for food became too intense or a change in the climate began to make their survival questionable, they would just gather up their weapons and tools and move to a more promising region, which explains why their remains can be found across Eurasia.[9]

The average H. ergaster/erectus stood around 5 feet 6 inches tall and weighed well over 100 pounds. Even though their bodies were just as elongated as modern humans, their skeletons were thicker, making them very robust in their body features. Protected by a thin coat of wiry hair and ebony colored skin, they walked with a slightly stooped back and a lethargic gait. Resting on top of their semi-broad shoulders was an elliptical-shaped head that revealed a flat face with a broad nose, a powerful jaw, and a set of small human-like teeth that were concealed behind a pair of wide lips. Across their sloping foreheads was a protruding brow ridge bone that projected a pair of dark penetrating eyes, which must have given them a very ferocious and unforgiving appearance.[10]

Overall, their facial features were still somewhat ape-like and yet their facial expressions and their body movements were probably very human. In terms of their physical stature, they were undoubtedly unimpressive as compared to the later-day humans. And yet, they were very strong, quick, and agile for their size. Individually, they weren't very threatening to the larger carnivores. But as an organized group of hunters, they must have been very intimidating.[11]

In due course, the H. ergaster/erectus migrated out of Africa and into Asia proper and then eventually into Europe. Initially, small groups of them ventured into the northern steppes of Eurasia and follow the great herds of animals eastward into northern Asia. As northern nomads, they were extremely mobile and dependent upon hunting the larger game. Meanwhile, the majority of them followed the coastlines into the various jungles, deep river valleys, and coastal plains in southern Asia. By hunting, gathering food, and fishing for their sustenance, these southern hunter-gatherers, as opposed to the northern nomadic hunters, would stake out the less accessible regions of Eurasia, thus forming their own territories.[12]

Although, these southern hunter-gatherers didn't follow the vast herds of animals in the northern steppes, they were still constantly on the move in search of plentiful game and richer surroundings. Thus, the size and the location of their territories were always changing, due to either drought, over-hunting, or unwelcome invaders. As part of the restless collection of early hominids, they weren't the nomadic wanderers in the strictest sense of the word. But, they were mainly hunters that had fully embraced the nomad's hunting skills and their culture. Rarely encountering their nomadic cousins of the northern steppes, except during a glaciation period, it was these southern hunter-gatherers' direct descendants, the Homo sapiens, that would one day evolve into the many different ethnic groups that we recognize today. But more importantly, and even less known, they would also become the first humans to till the land and form villages.[13]

For almost 2 million years, the H. ergaster/erectus hunted, scavenged, or gathered whatever food was available to them as they moved to more bountiful regions. Hardy, shrewd, energetic, resourceful, and organized, it didn't take very long before they became the lords of their surroundings. For unlike the H. habilis, they were predominately carnivorous hunters, who had become completely erect in their movements. Physically able to survive in almost every type of environment, they possessed the needed weaponry, along with the necessary cognitive, communication, and organizational skills to hunt the larger animals. And due to these unique abilities, they were able to hunt and devour into extinction almost any species within their reach, including quite possibly, their own distant relatives the australopithecines and the H. habilis.[14]

Scientists and scholars from all over the world are still attempting to answer the age old question as to how and why we evolved into much an intelligent and imaginative species. Certainly, our ability to change our economies has propelled our physical and cultural evolution, but it doesn't explain the development of our reasoning power, which gave us the ability to seek out new economies and form new societies. Hence, there must have been an ever-present physiological and cerebral stimulation occurring that made our ancestors' journeys possible and helped develop their unique mental and verbal abilities.

After our primate ancestors had left the dwindling forests of eastern Africa and began scavenging, there began a mutual stimulation between the working of their hands and minds that created an "evolutionary feedback loop." It was this self-perpetuating feedback loop that would eventually increase our ability to reason and thus our ability to form languages.

First as scavengers and then later as nomads, our ancestors were continuously working their hands and minds towards making better weapons and tools in order to improve their hunting skills. It was during this mutual beneficial process that they developed the ability to imagine new ideas, which would ultimately lead them to form verbal sounds to express those new ideas. As a consequence, this increased ability to imagine new ideas and form verbal sounds would further stimulate the use of their hands and minds on an even higher level.[15]

In other words, as our ancestors' hands became more agile and skilled in the process of making better weapons and tools, the process itself generated the development of their thought processes and that of their verbal skills, which would in turn stimulate an increase in the use of their hands and minds. This evolutionary relationship between working our hands, minds, and verbal skills slowly increased our ancestors' mental and verbal capabilities to the point where our ancestors would become destined to eventually domesticate the plants and animals.[16]

In addition to this initial evolutionary feedback loop, there also exists another aspect to their amazing mental and physical development: a second more substantial and broader loop.

While our ancestors' hands, minds, and verbal skills were constantly stimulating each other, as in the initial evolutionary feedback loop, their bodies developed a demand for more nutrition in order to keep up with their expanded exertions. This increase in the body's nutritional requirements stimulated an additional need for them to increase the use of their hands, mind, and verbal skills. As a result, the more nutrition they required, the harder they worked their hands, minds, and language skills in order to obtain that needed nutrition, thus establishing a perpetual cycle of expanding our species mental and verbal growth.

Since we began our incredible evolution as primordial anthropoid apes, these dual evolutionary feedback loops undoubtedly took a very long time to develop our mental and verbal abilities. However, they still exist with us today. In fact, they appear to be intensifying in their impact upon our evolution. Being a unique phenomenon of nature, these escalating cycles of expanding our mental and verbal abilities has the potential of eventually altering our species into a completely different looking species with unlimited cerebral powers. Several thousand years from now, it is doubtful that we would even recognize our own species. In the future, we'll probably evolve into another form of humanoid with a larger brain, bigger eyes, elongated fingers, a smaller set of teeth, and very little body hair. As long as we don't interrupt these evolutionary loops through some self-inflicted catastrophe such as global warming, nuclear or biological warfare, overpopulation, financial greed and corruption, or an environmental upheaval, the pace of our mental and physical evolution will continue to accelerate.

Even before the H. ergaster/erectus had begun to migrate into Asia, they already possessed a large assortment of Acheulean/Clactonian tools. By that time, they were quite capable of molding or chipping a variety of woods, stones, animal bones, and antlers into a number of useful weapons and tools. Their most important weapon/tool was a bifacial hand axe or cleaver. Employed as a versatile tool, the hunter could use it for many different purposes, including the chopping, hammering, scraping, dicing, smashing, peeling, sticking, and the slicing of whatever types of meats, fruits, leaves, roots, berries, or nuts that were available to them.[17]

However in order for the H. ergaster/erectus to have succeeded as nomads and move throughout Asia, they had to have possessed a better weapon system than just a hand-held rock. The simple act of throwing a stone flaked axe, no matter how many hunters were throwing it, wouldn't have been sufficient enough to kill the larger game. Thus, they were possibly the first hominids to make and then use the common spear, which would have been used for either throwing or plunging.[18]

By shaping the end of a long tree branch with a fire-tipped point, this simple weapon ensured their success in whichever continent they chose to inhabit. Moreover, the idea of producing a spear wouldn't have been a great technological leap for them to make, since their scavenging ancestors had already discovered the importance of being able to scare away a predator by using a long branch. Nevertheless, it probably didn't take very long before they began to replace the fire-tipped method with a bifacial stone, as indicted by the discovery of several Acheulean stone points in the West Turkana region of Kenya. Discovered by a French-led archaeology team, these particular points were dated to about 1.76 million years ago. Hence by the time the H. ergaster/erectus had migrated out of Africa, they were fairly sophisticated in their economic skills as compared to the H. habilis. It is by no mere coincidence that today's social scientists classify the our past civilizations by the type of tools they had constructed, because it is a direct indication of their level of economic and cultural achievement.[19]

The archaeological evidence appears to be highly circumstantial and continues to be debated as to when the H. ergaster/erectus actually began to use the amazing power of fire. Many of today's scientists believe it was somewhere between 800,000 to 1.8 million years ago that our ancestors first began to utilize this natural phenomenon, while many others believe it was somewhere around 400,000 years ago. Undoubtedly, this debate will continue for a very long time.[20]

Still and all, the use of controlled fire could have easily aided and even enabled our ancestors to migrate out of Africa and across Eurasia. During their long journeys, it would have given them another means of protecting themselves by using a torch to scare away the other predators. Also, they could have used the torches to hunt at night or to occupy the vacant caves throughout the mountain regions. The concept of creating a fire by rubbing two sticks together or by producing sparks with two pieces of flint in all likelihood came about much later in our evolution. Since these early hominids were probably incapable of producing a flame, they could have continuously carried around a crude hearth or a torch, so as to keep the flame going. But whatever the circumstances, it was a major evolutionary leap for our ancestors. It allowed them many advantages beyond just keeping themselves warm.

Initially, the power of the flame was most possibly made available to the H. ergaster/erectus by the bush fires that had been ignited by the occasional lightning storm or even by a nearby volcanic lava spill. Being a shrewd and an adaptable creature, it wouldn't have taken them very long to realize the many benefits of harnessing this awesome power. In fact, it also enabled them to venture out into the colder climate of Eurasia, where immensely large herds of animals had roamed. And quite frankly, life in the colder northern areas would have been impossible for them to have endured without the assistance of a controlled heat. This alone would have a tremendous impact upon their nomadic lives by permitting them to follow the herds evermore northward.[21]

Undeniably, the use of a camp fire had a profound effect upon their daily lives. Not only did fire protect our ancestors from the predators and kept them warm during the cold night, but it also greatly improved their daily diets. By the simple act of cooking their food, especially the meat, they were able to reduce the harmful effects of consuming parasites, toxins, and unwanted pathogens. Moreover, it would have invariably enabled them to adsorb more calories from their existing food by reducing the caloric cost of digestion. As a result of eating cooked and thus softer foods, our ancestors' jaw muscles would no longer have to support their huge jaws, which permitted their skulls to become larger and less compact, hence providing more room for a larger brain.[22]

But more importantly, the use of a camp fire must have had a perpetuating social impact towards our evolution by unknowingly encouraging a greater interaction between our ancestors. Huddled around the warm flames of an open fire undoubtedly aided the development of their language skills by further boosting their groups' behavioral inclination towards communicating and cooperating with each other.[23]

As a hereditary and cultural offspring of the earlier scavenging societies, the H. ergaster/erectus was an accumulation of well-over 3 million years of hominid development. While being fairly creative and skilled, they would take the nomadic economy to new heights. This was not only accomplished by their development of the Acheulean/Clactonian tool industry and their use of fire, but also by their ability to travel great distances.

Approximately 500,000 years ago as they migrated into the northern regions of Asia, our ancestors possibly began wearing clothing in the form of animal pelts. Besides insulating them against the cold, it also protected them from the harsh rain and biting sleet, rash-causing plants, insect bites, thorns, and the sun's harmful rays by providing a barrier between their skin and the elements. In the beginning, they might have just draped a pelt across their shoulders like a cape and just let it hang to their knees. Or they just sliced a hole into a pelt and then stuck their arms and legs through it. Similar to the construction of their temporary shelters that were made from grass, bushes, and tree branches, the act of wearing clothing would have enabled them to survive in the most inhospitable climates. Unlike the hominids before them, the H. ergaster/erectus had become so adaptable in their economic skills and in their cultural flexibility that it would take a lot more than just another glaciation period to erase their way of life.[24]

Generally speaking, the nomadic ruling structure was a classic patriarchy in the strictest sense. Ruled by men for the purpose of their benefit and pleasure, the culture was predominantly masculine in its configuration. This male orientated culture initially evolved out of their innate physiological advantage (sexual dimorphism) over their female counterparts. In terms of the males' greater body size, physical strength, and endurance, the females couldn't economically compete with them, when it came to hunting the big game, moving over long distances, or waging a war in order to protect their territories. And since the females' main responsibility was to bear children and protect the den, they weren't in position to economically dominate their societies. Within their roaming communities, the male members carried the primary economic responsibility for their livelihood and for their defense. If the males failed in these tasks, the band would become extinct. As a result, the nomadic males possessed and exercised the economic prerogative to politically rule their cultures.[25]

Another reason the H. ergaster/erectus was so hugely successful was their ability to better organize themselves with their improved communication skills. Whether their organizational skills initiated the improvement of their language skills or vice versa will never be known. But instead of continuing to form loosely knitted bands, like the australopithecines and the H. habilis before them, they would begin to combine several bands into larger and better-organized groups called clans, which were under the firm leadership of a single dominant male and his lieutenants.

Over a space of time, these clan leaders were able to communicate their commands in a more concise authoritarian manner by using simple sounds or syllables, and thus upholding their right to rule. In all probability, the H. ergaster/erectus couldn't form a complete sentence, a phrase, or maybe even a word. But today, it is believed by many scientists that they did possess a human voice, which indicates they could get their point across by employing various simple sounds, syllables, or even physical gestures. Undoubtedly, it was another major step in our evolution, because it would set the precedent for their future descendants to eventually form words, sentences, and then distinct languages.[26]

When our ancestors first began to organize their hunting societies, they unknowingly created the social basis of individual power, hence the basis for individual status. The competition for the leadership of the clan was intense as the hunters attempted to prove their dominance over the others. The individual's dominance over the other clan members was paramount in the delegation of authority and in the development of an organized group. In essence, the first clans established the authority of their chosen leader, all in the name of organizing their efforts to hunt. It was the simplest solution to the complex problem of leading a hunt or ruling a clan. Working within the scheme of a social hierarchy, the authority figure would become an essential element in organizing a successful hunting culture. Afterwards, a clan's time and energy were never wasted, so long as an authority figure controlled the process. As expected, the most successful clans were the most organized and authority driven.[27]

While following the great herds in the north or living as southern hunter-gatherers, it had become an economic necessity for the clans to centralize and intensify their governing structure for the purpose of increasing their efficiency as hunters, hence enabling them to react to the ever-changing circumstances as a cohesive body of one. Over the span of time, the leader would become a more forceful individual, who was expected to uphold the needed discipline and singular direction within the clan. With the expansion of his responsibilities and with the assistance of his loyal lieutenants, he began to ruthlessly demand a higher state of obedience and unity within his clan in order for them to survive the many hardships. If he had to punish an individual for his or her failing to conform, then it was within his authority to do so.

These Lower Paleolithic ruling bodies were simple organizations that brought about a degree of political order, security, and economic success within their restless societies. Although, the leader's authority was extremely limited, he was still considered the most important figure in directing the clan's energy towards a more centralized effort. If the clan needed to move to another region, form a hunting party, or establish a new camp site, he was the one that led the way. Thus through the establishment of a single leader and the new established social structure of the clan, we would take another giant leap towards ensuring our success as a species by establishing ourselves as an organized group and therefore indomitable in our pursuits.

It would be a huge mistake for anyone to believe that the institution of government was initially created once we began to till the soil and build our villages. In actuality, the establishment of the nomadic authority figure was the genesis of our later-day governments. By this very act of proclaiming a sole leader, the nomads were unknowingly setting the precedent for creating a ruling body with the power to rule. From this point onwards, the clans' leader and his loyal lieutenants were responsible for the defense, lawfulness, and the welfare of its people, which happens to be the main duties and responsibilities of today's national, state, and local governments.

The H. ergaster/erectus ability to emotionally express themselves had been handed down to them by their primate ancestors of the great forests. As wanderers competing with the other nomadic clans, the ability to laugh, to cry, and to express anger would have temporarily released the mental, emotional, and physical pressures that had accumulated during their survival experiences. However, the very human expressions of remorse, hatred, apathy, and boredom, just to name a few, probably didn't become a significant part of our behavioral patterns until we had become more intimate with each other by forming family units. Accordingly, this would inevitably lead to the improvement of our language skills by the need to communicate and emotionally express ourselves to the others around us. Of course, there are many different theories as to the purposes behind such expressive behaviors. But, there can be no denying the fact that as a highly social and emotional species, the need for personal intimacy would become progressively more pronounced, once we had become nomads and began to form our own family units.

It's not entirely known when our ancestors took the first giant step towards forming actual family units. But, it must have been around the time the H. ergaster/erectus were in the process of migrating into Asia. As a consequence, the old primate social structure of an individual living within his or her gender group would have given way to the economic pressures to form a functional family. Unfortunately, we can only guess as to its subsequent development.

Stretching back to the early stages of our evolution, our relationships had been based upon a fission-fusion arrangement (cenogamy), where everyone was bonded to his or her own gender group. The concept of a male permanently bonding with female hadn't yet emerged. And yet, the leader (alpha male) of the band and his favorite alpha female did form a special relationship called pair-bonding. This relationship was essentially a mutual obligation between the two most dominant individuals within their respective genders. They weren't married in the modern sense of the word, but they did form a special bond. Besides protecting, caressing, and grooming each other, they would ensure each other's survival by sharing their food, warmth, and on occasion their sleeping arrangements. Even though they were free to seek out other companions, their first allegiance was to each other.[28]

Once our ancestors had become successful northern nomads and southern hunter-gatherers, the cultural dynamics of their roaming clans underwent a dramatic change. As earlier food gatherers and scavengers, the distribution of food was carried out through the social hierarchy, depending upon where the individual stood within his or her own gender group. For instance, once the males had killed a prey, the females and their offspring were usually forced to beg for whatever meat was left over. This type of food distribution system had worked very well in the past within the jungles and the thick forests, where the females and their offspring were free to find their own food among the tall trees and bushes. But as they began to venture out onto the barren savannas, the females were expected to stay behind and protect the children. As a result, this system had become totally outdated, thus leaving the women and their children extremely vulnerable to undernourishment and even starvation.[29]

As the males improved their ability to hunt, there appeared a wide discrepancy between the individual hunters ability to provide food on a consistent basis. Much like a bell curve within any modern classroom, a small percentage of the males (alphas) had become very efficient at hunting due to their superior physical and mental skills, while another small percentage (omegas) were very inept. Meanwhile, the overall majority of them (betas) were just efficient enough to be called average. Within their small clans, it would have become common knowledge among the members which individual hunters were the most successful in hunting and providing them meat. Accordingly, the individual females would begin seeking out those males efficient enough at hunting and social status to provide them and their offspring with an adequate amount of food throughout the whole year. Thus, this simple act of expanding the pair-bonding to include the clans' betas and omegas was a direct response to their need to establish a more efficient food distribution system.[30]

Presumably, this act of pair-bonding and the altering of their food distribution system began to change their sleeping arrangements. Instead of the females huddling around the alpha males as they had done in the past, the young females would begin to crawl next to one of the more numerous beta males during the night as a source of warmth, protection, and the possibility of finding a provider. If the male was agreeable to her presence by not rejecting her, they would continue to sleep together and begin to pair-bond through the acts of sharing their food, grooming each other, and procreating.

Needless to say, this change in their sleeping arrangements would have had a profound effect upon intensifying our interpersonal relationships. Ultimately, it formed our first single family units, whereupon the female would begin to exclusively depend upon the male for her security and sustenance in exchange for her becoming his sexual possession and caretaker of their children. Of course, the more dominant and efficient hunters could find themselves sleeping with more than one female, hence the birth of polygamy. But whatever the circumstances, once a couple had pair-bonded, it was usually for life.[31]

As a result of pair-bonding, the majority of the females and their offspring weren't dependent upon the clan's leftover scraps any longer. Instead of suffering the effects of a strict pecking order, the males would take their portion of the freshly killed carcass and then share it with their new found female partner or partners. Then, the females would in turn share it with their hungry offspring. Consequently, the overwhelming majority of our early ancestors were able to eat on a consistent basis. It was a workable food distributing system that was born out of pure necessity. However, the omega males and females that normally bonded together would have had a hard time of it, unless the hunt had been a very successful affair.[32]

The appearance of the family unit not only helped to develop a new food distribution system through the act of pair-bonding, but it also helped to serve their population needs as well. Within the scattered and isolated clans, the ratio between the number of males and females was rarely equal. Thus, our nomadic ancestors were forced to make allowances for this disparity by forming many different types of family relationships.

Simply stated, whenever there was an overabundance of females, which was perhaps the norm; the males would take up the stack by acquiring another wife or even several wives. By forming a polygamous family unit, it ensured that everyone was fed and that their population would remain constant. Then on the other hand, whenever there was an overabundance of males, a female would pair-bond with a small group of males, thereupon forming a polyandry relationship. Of course, a polyandrous family relationship was a very rare occurrence among the nomads, due to the males' sexual possessiveness. Yet, it might have existed among the southern hunter-gatherers, where the food was more readily available to both genders. As for the monogamous relationship, it was usually present among the less dominant omegas and especially whenever the genders were almost equal in number.

Undeniably, this act of pair-bonding helped to induce our strong personal bonds between each other, which undoubtedly affected our sexual habits. Instead of the males physically positioning themselves behind the females, they would begin to copulate face to face as a ritual of mutual possession. Intensely more intimate and sexually satisfying for both parties, this simple act of sharing the pleasure and the need of procreation further deepened their feelings for each other and humanize their lives to a level unheard of within the animal kingdom. Today, we take these behaviors for granted. But at the time, they were remarkable revolutionary events for our future cultural development. They literally enabled us to stabilize the family unit by intensifying the personal intimacy between each other, while establishing for the first time, a mutually binding relationship between a man and a woman.[33]

As northern nomads, the H. ergaster/erectus developed a very successful hunting culture. In fact, their culture was so successful that they eventually roamed the earth supreme. After learning to hunt as an organized group, their survival was assured by simply following the great herds of migrating animals. During the winter months, they pursued them southward into the warmer areas, where the grass was still green. Then during the summer months, they would slowly follow them back northward to avoid the dry season. In spite of the fact that they were forced to practice infanticide throughout the most difficult times and they never hunted at night, their proficiency in hunting was so successful that their populations began to grow. As a result, some of the clans would eventually be forced to migrate into the other parts of Eurasia and Africa. But it does beg the question; how did our ancestors learn to hunt the larger animals? [34]

It wasn't very difficult for the H. ergaster/erectus to individually hunt the smaller game. The H. habilis before them had already perfected the many different hunting techniques. But the needed skills for centralized control (hierarchy), practical planning (symbols), and basic communication skills that were required to hunt as an effective group and bring down a large animal couldn't have been learned overnight. It could have taken millenniums.

In all probability, the H. ergaster/erectus began to learn the techniques of group hunting by observing and then emulating the different packs of marauding animals overcoming a much larger prey. By observing an alpha male evasively maneuvering his pack (e.g. wolves, jackals, hyenas etc.) into a position to attack an unsuspecting or injured animal, our ancestors would have been given a classic example of teamwork, mobility, deception, and surprise in action. To the hungry nomads, who understood the many benefits of hunting the big game, it must have been a very enlightening sight.

In a very real sense, it was these roaming packs of animals that were the catalyst of our ancestors becoming and then succeeding as northern nomads or as southern hunter-gatherers. In fact, it was another significant step in our evolution. The needed skills to hunt as a coordinated group couldn't have been learned through trial and error alone. While being creatures of imitation and habit, the H. ergaster/erectus would have learned how to hunt the big game and how to protect themselves against the larger predators by emulating the other animals' strategies.[35]

It is no small wonder that even today many people feel an indescribable kinship towards the animal kingdom. For not only did they provide us with the food and clothing in order to survive, they also showed us how to change our way of life. Instead of remaining the passive food gatherers and the scavengers of carcasses, the surrounding packs of animals had demonstrated to us the necessary tactics and skills to become an organized group of wandering hunters. Our ancestors already had a pecking order that established a leadership framework within each clan and the rudimentary hand signals or verbal sounds in which to communicate with each other; all they really needed was a method and a plan.[36]

Among the vast golden grasses of the Eurasian steppes, the landscape was intersected with rugged ravines, rising mesas, and shallow valleys. Many of the animals found relief from the scorching midday sun by resting under or around the clumps of the trees, dense shrubs, or near the isolated watering holes. Amid these shady havens, a variety of poisonous snakes, swarming insects and deadly predators also rested as they waited for sundown. Constantly moving from area to area in search of better grazing land, the great herds could suddenly disappear from the horizon as quickly as they had appeared. Thus hunting them throughout the vast hinterland was no simple task. Dangers could be lurking behind every bush and underneath every rock.

By learning the animals' feeding habits, these early nomads became extremely skilled at locating a herd on a fairly consistent basis. To the alert hunter, the dampness of their dung, the hint of freshly gnawed grass, and the impressions of their hoof prints were all indications of the animals' earlier presence and the direction in which they were moving. Even in the most rugged terrain, the hunters could identify an animal's peculiar mating call, the drifting scent of their body odors, or the stench of their urine. All it took was learning a few basic tracking skills. However, it would have taken a lot of skill and patience to bring down one of these huge animals. Invariably, the best trackers and hunters would begin to achieve a special status within their own clan, thus encouraging the individual to outperform the others.[37]

Since the northern nomads couldn't kill them at a great distance, they were forced to come up with a variety of different strategies. While being better organized than their ancestors, their hunting techniques were in all probability extremely simple and effective. The biggest problem facing our ancestors wasn't whether or not they could bring down a large animal. That could have been done fairly easily by surrounding a prey and then plunging their long fire-tipped wooden spears into the animal's vital parts. Instead, the biggest dilemma they faced in successfully hunting the roaming herds was twofold. Initially, they had to figure out a way to get close enough without alarming them.

Secondly, they had to figure out a way to isolate one of animals from the rest of the herd in order to have any chance of killing it.

Simply chasing a herd off a cliff or pursuing them in foot race until they became incapacitated through exhaustion (persistent hunting technique) might have solved their problem and was in all likelihood used by some of the clans, depending upon the type of terrain. But unfortunately, a stampeding herd can turn on a dime so as to avoid danger. While chasing a gazing animal might appear to be good idea at the time, the hunters never knew if they were unintentionally chasing the prey into a den of larger predators, thus turning themselves into the prey.

Undoubtedly, the northern nomads developed their own methods for hunting out on the steppes. By positioning themselves downwind from the unsuspecting animals, they could have concealed their approach either by moving along a dried-up riverbed or along a shallow ravine. In this manner, they were able to move within the general vicinity of the herd without giving them an opportunity to sense the approaching danger. Pausing just long enough to camouflage themselves by smearing mud and leaves or even animal dung all over their bodies, the hunters would then attempt to get as close as possible to them by slowly crawling along the ground. By moving ever so slowly and quietly, it was their intention to position themselves on the outer periphery of the herd so that they could form a wide semi-circle among the high grass or thick shrubs. This technique could have easily been learned by watching the lions and cheetahs hunting their prey.

It was at this point that they had to demonstrate a great degree of patience. While waiting for a single animal to wander into their ambush, they sometimes had to lie in the grass for hours on end. And if they were unlucky or unskilled, the herd would become startled and suddenly move off into another direction, thus leaving the disappointed hunters behind to hunt another day. But when one of the animals did enter the trap, the hunters would spring up from the ground and plunge their long fire-tipped spears into the prey's body. Since there was usually an average of 5 to 15 hunters on each hunting trip, the actual kill must have taken but a few minutes.

Since the southern hunter-gatherers lived and prospered throughout southern Eurasia, what had worked for their northern cousins out in the open steppes wouldn't have worked for them along the southern bush covered riverbanks, the coastal mountain ranges, or even the jungles and forests. And yet many of their tactics must have been based upon their ancestors' previous experiences. Centered mainly upon the ambush, they would employ the tactics of camouflage, concealment, surprise, and panic to their best advantage. Not surprisingly, they would eventually become skilled enough to hunt the most elusive animals within every type of terrain and weather.

As a rule of thumb, the herds naturally congregated around sources of water such as rivers, streams, or lakes. As a result, the southern hunter-gatherers could have used several different tactics. While concealing themselves in a semi-circle among the vegetation around these water sources, they would patiently wait for the herd to come to them. From their past experiences, they knew that the approaching animals would become excited by the smell of fresh water and begin pushing each other towards the source of refreshment. Invariably, a few of them ended up wandering up and down the banks looking for a point of entry into the cool water. It was at this critical point that one of the animals would stumble into the hunters' semi-circle. Then, it was just a question of the hunters following the leader's signal by springing the trap at the right moment.[38]

Besides chasing a herd into a box canyon and then throwing their spears into the animals from atop the cliffs, it was during the dry season that the H. ergaster/erectus might have employed another technique from observing the larger predators panic their prey into an ambush. It was a simple technique and ridiculously effective. As a thirsty herd was fast approaching the river, the concealed hunters would jump up from their hiding places situated behind the on-rushing herd and create a scene of total mayhem. By waving a hand-full of bushes or animal pelts in the air and screaming at the top of their lungs, the hunters were able to panic the herd into the shallow water by effectively using the animal's own momentum. Then once the herd had panicked and rushed into the river or along its bank, the hunters would either kill the unlucky ones that had found themselves stuck in the mud or ambush the ones that had run along bank.

While being extremely flexible in their eating habits, our ancestors must have consumed almost everything that walked, hopped, crawled, swam, or flew. In addition to eating a large assortment of seeds, wild fruits, roots, berries, leaves, tree bark, and even insects, they gorged themselves whenever possible on birds, fish, turtles, frogs, honey, small game, and any available eggs. Long before there were any established religious taboos about eating certain foods, our ancestors were free to eat whatever nourishment was available to them. And since their survival was at stake and the herds could sometimes disappear for weeks or even months on end, there wouldn't have been any moral code from preventing them from eating the most unimaginably foods from the most mind-bogglingly sources. In addition to eating every part of an animal, including its intestines, brain, eyes, testicles, and tongue, it was during the winter months that they would pick and eat the seeds from the surrounding animal dung or even consume the parasites from their own bodies.[39]

Once the H. ergaster/erectus had begun pair-bonding and forming loyal family units, they probably ceased to consume their own clan members during the hard and hungry times. But on the other hand, it might not have been beyond their disposition to consume a member from another clan. As predominant and indeed ruthless carnivores, the hunting and consumption of fresh meat was the basis of their nomadic economy and culture. Whether the meat came from an antelope or from another hominid wouldn't have made much difference to them within an extremely primitive and highly mobile culture. The eating of other forms of food such as plants, honey, berries, seeds, and roots, might have satisfied their hunger up to a certain point. But eventually, they would have turned to whatever source of meat that was available to fulfill their need for protein.[40]

There is ample evidence that the act of cannibalism was much more prevalent within our early hunting cultures than our modern scientists and scholars have cared to admit. However, there is a distinct possibly that it was beginning to become a taboo within the southern hunter-gatherers tribes (see chapter 4, page 57-58), once we had become Homo sapiens sapiens around 45,000 years ago. It was during this period that we were becoming more human and creative in our behaviors. But on the other hand, it probably didn't become an absolute taboo within our societies until after we had begun to domesticate the surrounding plants and animals. At that point, our prehistoric ancestors were in the middle of changing their eating habits from their previous nomadic days towards eating less meat and eating more grains, fruits, and vegetables. For the first time in our history, the individual's ability to produce food in the surrounding fields was far greater, than his or her value as a mere cadaver.[41]

And finally as our ancient histories have illustrated, this taboo for cannibalism within the early agrarian societies would take on an extreme religious and civic dimension. Since it had become morally and economically repugnant to the agrarians, these ancient cannibalistic nomads were ostracized, hunted down, and then exterminated by the far ranging armies of the farming societies. Eventually, these scattered nomads were forced to give up the practice in order to ensure their continued existence. Even in the present day, the remnants of these cannibalistic cultures can only be found in the most remote regions of the world, where they still practice a form of ritualistic cannibalism.

As nomadic hunters, these men and women were clothed in crude animal skins and carried their young children on their backs over long distances amid the unforgiving rain and freezing snow. They dwelled within the caves or under the trees, feasted on the burnt flesh of animals or roasted roots, groaned beneath the constant hunger, and pursued the game with a vengeance. And yet these early hunters continued to carve and fight their way through the wilderness, living a short and brutal life with having very little understanding of the forces around them. They had begun to plan and learn from the hard lessons of existence as they imparted that knowledge to the next generation. They were different than modern man and woman only in their profound ignorance, lack of creativeness, and primitive behaviors that had long been established among their blood-related clans. They lived in an unrelenting cycle of giving birth, roaming, hunting, killing, skinning, gutting, feasting, mating, and eventually dying. They knew hope, joy, love, fear, anger, envy, and despair. With well over one million years of biological development behind them, they had become incredibly adaptable and the most dangerous creatures on the planet.

Chapter Five

The Lower Paleolithic Nomads
"Homo heidelbergensis"

"We live between two worlds; we soar in the atmosphere; we creep upon the soil; we have the aspirations of creators and the propensities of quadrupeds. There can be but one explanation of this fact. We are passing from the animal into a higher form, and the drama of this planet is in its second act."

William Winwood Reade (1838-1875)
British Historian and Philosopher

As of today, there is some archaeological evidence that indicates the Homo antecessor is one of our direct ancestors. Making their appearance around 750,000 years ago, they are the oldest confirmed European hominids. They were almost 6 feet tall and weight close to 200 pounds with a brain size of around 1000cc. Many of their fossils possess marks from cutting, chopping, and striking by a stone tool, which is an indication that they were cannibalistically butchered and consumed by their own species. The mid-facial area of the H. antecessor seems very modern, but the other parts of the skull such as the teeth, forehead, and the brow ridges are exceedingly primitive. Physically more robust in stature as compared to the H. ergaster/erectus, many scientists are doubtful about the validity of the H. antecessor as a separate species, partly because, the archaeological evidence is based upon the remains of a few juvenile specimens. They insist the H. antecessor was really a European H. ergaster/erectus. At the same time, many other scientists believe they are the same species as the Homo heidelbergensis, which is also a real possibility. Thus whether or not the H. antecessor is a separate species or even one of our direct ancestors will probably be determined at a later date.[1]

Approximately 600,000 years ago, the Homo heidelbergensis (rhodesians) suddenly appeared as a more recognizable candidate in our ascension from the H. ergaster/erectus species. At the beginning of the Mindel-Riss interglacial period, they began to branch out into three other hominid species as a result of the natural selection pressures placed upon the survivors of the previous Mindel glaciation period. Presently, the DNA comparisons indicate that the H. s neanderthalensis, the Denisovans, and that of our own species, the Homo sapiens, were their direct descendants. Whereas, the chromosomal evidence reveals that the H. heidelbergensis split off into two groups after leaving Africa in between 300,000 to 400,000 years ago. One group eventually evolved into the European Neanderthals, while the other one became the Asian Denisovans. In addition, it is believed that our own African Homo sapiens had diverged from them around 200,000 years ago. If this is the case, then that would render the H. heidelbergensis the forerunners of several later-day hominid species.[2]

Standing in between 4 feet 9 inches to 6 feet tall and possessing a very muscular body weighing over 150 pounds, the H. heidelbergensis brain was almost the size (1274cc) of modern humans (1350cc). Their skeleton and teeth were less robust than the H. ergaster/erectus, but more robust than modern humans. Moreover, their skulls had a large brow ridge, a sloping forehead, and a receding chin. The physiological evidence also indicates that they were the first hominids to speak a primitive language. Without a doubt, these archaic humans were a very important link to our evolution. Definitely more sophisticated in their organizational skills from our previous ancestors; their main contribution towards our species' advancement would be within the realm of further establishing our basic family roles and social structure.[3]

Somewhere around 500,000 years ago, these early H. heidelbergensis were in all likelihood the first hominids to make a controlled fire. In the past, the major problem in keeping a fire alive was that it had to be continuously fed by someone. During the rainy season, this must have been a very difficult task to achieve. Nevertheless, it must have been an accident waiting to happen. While in the process of making bifacial chipped weapons and tools, the sparks from the flints could have easily ignited a nearby patch of dry grass. And since our nomadic ancestors were frequently making stone and flint implements, the production of sparks must have been an everyday affair.[4]

As the H. heidelbergensis gathered around the smoky camp fire, it would have been a common practice for them to throw a wide variety of meats, roots, berries, fruits, nuts, and insects onto the hot embers for roasting. While enjoying the different aromas drifting through the night air, it was moments like these that were the high point of their day, momentarily safe from the dangers around them, while feasting on their hot meals. As a consequence, this nightly ritual of cooking and consuming their meals not only improved their language skills and their thought processes through the exchanging of ideas, experiences, and emotions, but it would have also inspired their imaginations as well.

Still, the most mysterious aspect of our discovery of fire was in the realm of mysticism. The veneration of fire is one of the oldest forms of human worship. Recognized as a manifestation of a divinity or a particular spirit by the later-day nomads, the flames represented a source of adoration and reverence. Since it was the first form of energy that humans could actually create and control, the nomads deified it. In their minds, it must have been a gift from one of the spiritual powers around them. Later in almost every agrarian mythology, there was an ancient account of how fire was given to their people by the gods in order to enhance their power and to provide them with both physical and spiritual light. Even in modern times, some religions still use fire as part of their purification rite or as a symbolic force of redemption. Amazingly, the flickering flame of an outdoor campfire still continues to this day to have a mesmerizing effect upon the young and old alike.[5]

Due to their wandering economy, the social structure of the early nomadic family became a very unique arrangement. Enduring the many hardships and dangers, they began to develop an intense group relationship between their family members that is almost completely unknown in the urban communities of today. Consisting of a small fiercely devoted collection of kinfolk within the clan, the extended nucleus family was made-up of moms and dads, brothers and sisters, aunts and uncles, nieces and nephews, and occasionally grandparents. They were taught since early childhood that the individual's obedience, cooperation, and loyalty to the family were all important. No doubt, they had personal conflicts between the individuals like most families experience in modern times. But amid an extremely hostile and unforgiving environment, they would bond together and form a ring of steel among themselves in order to overcome the challenges of the day. Thus, their whole world evolved around the people whose blood ran through their veins and the individuals they called their own.

Within every nomadic family, the members were irreversibly tied to a social order and to the success of the clan. The idea of an individual or a young couple striking out on their own was completely alien to them. Survival on the blistering plains or in the deep forests was tough enough for a large group of people, but for individuals, it was almost impossible. Thus as kindred spirits, they were expected to fulfill and maintain their social positions within the family unit. Controlled by the stagnation and severity of their clan traditions, the concept of Western individualism didn't exist within their conscious minds. The needs of the family, along with the needs of the clan, were considered far more important than the individual's needs. Subsequently, their own personal identity and that of their relationships with others were centered upon the belief that they existed within a circle of people. And as a part of that circle, they never spoke, acted, or responded as individuals, but rather as ambassadors of their past lineage.[6]

The negative repercussions of incest were either unknown or undoubtedly ignored altogether as a consequence of living within a limited number of people. The choice of mates was naturally restricted within an economy that didn't encourage peaceful interaction with the other nomadic clans. It was by no mere coincidence that giving birth to a baby boy was considered a great asset. Nomadic life was harsh and demanding, thus necessitating the desire for as many males as possible. When infanticide was performed, during the most meager of times, it was the baby girls and the weak sickly boys that were usually sacrificed.

Undoubtedly, this must have been a very heart-breaking experience for such a close-knit group.[7]

Despite the fact that the average life span of a nomad was around 30 years old, the older members of the clan were revered for their wisdom and insight, so long as they hadn't become a hindrance. Tragically, once a family member had become too old or too ill to keep up with the rest of the wandering clan, he or she would be left behind in the dust. This form of indifference towards the old and medically unfit was a necessary evil in order for the nomadic economy to function at a very high level. Again, the leaving behind of a loved one must have been very distressing to everyone. Yet, if the children were expected to have any chance of survival, it had to be done.[8]

Remarkably, this ancient nomadic attitude towards the old and ailing can be observed even within our industrial times. In contrast to leaving them behind on the trail, it is quite common for today's families to move their aged relatives to a nursing home in the hopes of providing them with better care. Yet the agrarian extended families were the exact opposite. They would care for their family members until the day they died, no matter what their age or physical condition. While farming and herding for a living, their value systems had evolved around their blood kin of the nucleus family unit and the profound interdependent relationships that had developed between them. Unfortunately, when it comes to fulfilling our industrial obligations by keeping up with the Joneses, a lot of people within the larger cities won't let the sanctity of their family relationships stand in the way of them maintaining a modern lifestyle.[9]

With the rise of the H. heidelbergensis, the social status within their nomadic societies became centered upon an individual's ability to contribute something toward the survival of the clan. For the typical male, his main responsibilities were to produce nourishment (game), protect the clan, and to sire as many offspring as possible. Raised to endure the many hardships, he was lean, agile, robust, and above all, sexually prolific. Yet in response to the rise of the family unit through the act of pair-bonding, a new and very significant role emerged within the family. It was a role that would have a tremendous impact upon our future cultures; a role that would come to dominate our later-day agrarian societies. Thus within the stark realities of their world, the role of the father figure would slowly emerge to become a very important part of our success.[10]

As father figures, the men provided the young males with the guidance and the instruction they needed to successfully ensure the clans survival. It was from their patient instruction that these sons would soon learn how to track and then to bring down the big game. Overall, the father's influence upon the children was very different, but no less profound than that of the mother's. Standing aloof from the everyday chores of maintaining a campsite and raising the younger children, these patriarchs of mobility would have not only transferred the skills of their survival, but also the importance of their clan's traditions and laws. Through the use of demonstrations, simple instructions, and modeling, it was the fathers' responsibility to convey to each generation of hunters the miracle of the flame, the power of the weapon, and the importance of cooperation.

Initially, the young boys received their instructions from their fathers in the making and the handling of their crude weapons. Once this was accomplished, they were then shown how to track and then bring down their prey. These lessons were usually accomplished by taking the boys out on short hunting trips. It was during these trips that they were also taught the discipline and coordination that it takes to function as an effective group. And like boys everywhere, the occasional rap on the noggin had to be applied in order to get their attention.

With the emergence of the role of the father and the already established role of the mother, these wandering humans became the founders of the first human institution, the institution of education. As parents, they would establish the cultural mechanism that has continuously transferred the necessary knowledge, skills, values, traditions, and the methods of our survival from one generation to another. It started out as it does every day in today's societies; an incredible process beginning with the very moment a child comes into this world. Not surprisingly, it is a process far more important to our survival than any other institution that exists in modern times. In fact without it, our species would still be clinging to the trees. Hence contrary to popular myth, it wasn't the role of the hunter, the warrior, or even the prostitute that became the first human profession, it was the teacher.[11]

It was sometime during this period that our male ancestors were forced to learn another role in their struggle for survival. Besides fulfilling the role of the hunter and father, they were also expected to perform the role of the warrior. This new role would come about due to the tremendous success of the nomadic economy and the expansion of the archaic human population. Among the grassy prairies, the meandering river valleys, and the moist lowlands, their populations steadily grew and began to spread across the landscape. During the spring and summer months, they could expect to find a wide variety of food in the form of fattened animals, edible roots, wild berries, and flowering plants. But in the winter months, they could face long periods of starvation and thus disease. Inevitably though, these roaming clans would begin to meet and then confront each other over the richest areas to hunt. Therefore, the role of the warrior would eventually become just as important, if not more so, than that of the everyday hunter.[12]

The Lower Paleolithic societies were based upon the male's ability to hunt the larger game, while protecting their precious families from the surrounding dangers. For the individual male, the possibility of obtaining a heightened social status within the clan would become the driving force behind his nomadic lifestyle. Within their temporary campsites, the constant glorification and reinforcement of the masculine qualities would help promote their success within an ever hostile and competitive environment.

The nomadic male had unwaveringly learned to become a husband, a father, a hunter, and a warrior, but above all he was a killer by instinct. While consuming the flesh of animals and wearing their furs, he would come to worship their mysterious spirits. As a sign of his own mystical power, he would begin to decorate himself with their teeth, bones, feathers, claws, and skulls. Never fully trusting or understanding the whims of the spirits, he walked over the landscape forming steadfast and life-long friendships with his fellow hunters. Unified in both purpose and deeds, they had the audacity and determination to stand against the world and bay at the moon. As true men and protectors of the dens, they invaded much of the world as conquerors. Erect, cautious, self-assured, and possessing the necessary weapons and tools, they had marched through time as prehistoric hunters. They lived for the ecstasy of the pursuit, the elation of the kill, the euphoria of the victorious hunter's return, and the gorging of the communal feast. And when they weren't dominating the world, they felt the joy of a woman's presence, the agony of a starving child, and the fulfillment of a successful hunt.

As for the H. heidelbergensis female, her unique qualities were revered within the clans. However, she was usually excluded from fulfilling the man's dual role of the hunter and warrior. For the sake of their clans' genetic and cultural continuance, she was needed to bare and then raise their children in order to maintain their population. Thus, the female wasn't encouraged, nor was she expected to participate in either the hunt or the war parties. And yet, she would fight and die, as well as any male, to defend her children and the clan's campsite from any marauding raiders.

Within the clans, a female's social status was based upon her ability to procreate children, gather food, protect and maintain the camp site, heal the sick, and perform a wide variety of other valuable services. These services included such responsibilities as healing the sick, teaching the young females, collecting fire wood, preparing the food, constructing the temporary shelters, and caring for her children and her mate. Then much later as the nomadic societies evolved, she would also be expected to produce the family's goods in the form of blankets, baskets, toys, belts, foot wear, clothing, and jewelry. Hence, it wasn't uncommon for a particular older female to possess great power and respect among the clan and her peers. Similar to their primate ancestors, the women of the clan also had their own pecking order. Positioned below the most dominant female, the other females were expected to prove their worth to the other women of the clan, before they could receive any degree of social status.

On a political level, an individual female's influence upon the clan's decision-making process was limited at best. But as a unified group, their opinions carried a lot of weight with the men. Overall, the cultural value of the female within the clan and her family was immense. Within any past or present human civilization, females have always been the guardians of the society's culture. By their very nature, they have consciously preserved our sacred traditions and cultural achievements by persistently transferring them to the next generation in an effort to maintain our way of life. Whether they accomplished this through their art, oral histories, or through their modeling behaviors, the cultural effect would be everlasting. In terms of teaching the children values, acceptable behaviors, and customs, the mothers' contribution to the clan was invaluable to their success. In modern times, societies tend to overlook the incalculable contribution of the role of the mother. Unquestionably, there is nothing more necessary and influential, than a mother who rears her children during their most impressionable years. Without their steady influences, our cultures would have quickly disappeared into a forgotten past.

While always living on the move, the mothers instructed the young females on the many different skills that it would take to survive. Through unwearied instruction and constant practice, the young females were taught how to prepare a campsite, care for the sick and injured, and stitch together the animal hides for making clothing and temporary shelters. And when they weren't being taught the different types of berries, nuts, and fruits to pick, the best types of firewood to collect, or how to roast a meal, they were shown the needed skills to rear their children and to assist the other females in childbirth. Within each clan, it was the mothers' responsibility to counsel the young females about the many different pair-bonding problems that could arise and their place within the clan. As the keepers of the clan's traditions and customs, these indomitable and inspirational women would pass on the stories about the greatness of their clan and the ever-ceasing need to produce more children.

The nomadic women were born and raised for a life of servitude. While being a part of a patriarchal nomadic culture, theirs was a life of constant hardship, sacrifice, and toil. It was a life where they were forced to be a second class citizen. Yet to the nomadic woman, there was a sense of balance about it all. Within her mind-set, the male's dominant role as the main provider would free her to perform the equally important tasks of maintaining the culture, the campsite, and caring for the children. Since she and her children's survival were primarily dependent upon the male's masculine abilities, she accepted her all-important function of supporting her man's position. In a very real sense, his pride was her pride and his success was her success. Thus, the more powerful and the more respected her mate had become within the clan; the more powerful and respected she became.

Throughout their short lifespans, the females bared their children and cared for the camp. They lived for the preservation of their traditions, the warmth of a child's smile, the rapture of a mate's embrace, and the gratification of watching her children grow into adults and continuing their way of life. As true women and creators of the dens, they fulfilled a thousand different and important tasks, rarely healthy and always helpful to those in need. They were stoically and patiently courageous in all of their endeavors. They were the glue that held the clan together and made life bearable for everyone. And while sharing their fate with the men, they felt the joy of love, the tenderness of belonging, and the horrible anguish of losing a loved one.

As different genders, we have developed our own unique strengths, weaknesses, and emotional characteristics. While being almost completely opposite in our values, perceptions, yearnings, and needs, it sometimes appears as if we are two different species altogether, which didn't go unnoticed by our ancient scholars. Within ancient Chinese lore, the male's masculine principle of "yang" represented the fire born from the sun and the energy it releases. Crude, forceful, and emotionally remote, the nomadic male would eventually conquer and dominate every corner of the planet with his spears and axes. Much like an uncontrollable beast, he reveled in its violence, its challenges, its alleged glory, and in its camaraderie that can only be found among men.[13]

In contrast, the female's feminine principle of "yin" represented the flexibility and elusiveness of water that flows from the earth's oceans and rivers, thus engulfing the fire and taming the male beast. Discreet, persuasive, and compassionate, the women would follow their men to the ends of the earth, mending their wounds and bearing their children. As steadfast and loyal companions, they gleamed in its raw excitement, its perceived grandeur, and its poignant relationships.[14]

On their own, the early men and women couldn't have survived the struggles of existence without each other's assistance. As separate genders, we would have perished with the first catastrophe. But as a family unit, we have become an indomitable and irresistible force, which can move mountains, conquer the unknown, and dream the unbelievable. Thus, it is by no mere coincidence that this dualistic nature of our species has extended from our families and into our cultures as well.

Within every past and present human society, there has existed two very different and distinctive types of social patterns, or rather subcultures. Individually, they represent extremely powerful forces that have revealed themselves in almost every form of human endeavor. Due to the differences in our genders' physical characteristics, behavioral patterns, value systems, emotional needs, self-perceptions, and even our fantasies, these two subcultures were initially established by our primate ancestors in the forests of eastern Africa as a consequence of their gender groupings. Thus, the individuals that have predominately encompassed our masculine (patri-culture) characteristics represent one of these subcultures; while the individuals that have predominately encompassed our feminine (matri-culture) characteristics have represented the other.[15]

Although, these two subcultures are attracted to each other for totally different reasons and strive to cooperate with each other out of economical and biological necessity, there exists an unrelenting conflict between them. In a very real sense, this conflict is revealed and sustained by their day to day interaction. Consciously or not, they are continuously struggling against each other for the cultural supremacy of their society. Hence, this power struggle can be observed within every corner of human society. And yet, it does serve a positive evolutionary purpose. As a cultural manifestation of the subcultures different goals, values, and priorities, the conflict is actually an internal process that maintains our societies' success through its continuous reexamination and eventual agreement of our economic and cultural objectives in an ever-changing world.[16]

Since we react differently to the individuals within the other subculture, while relating to those in our own, these conflicting relationships between the individuals of the two subcultures could be described as a major component of the inner dynamics of human culture. It is a competitive, disruptive, informative, and a creative process that is ever-present and almost always beneficial in revealing our different options during times of extreme uncertainty. Moreover, it not only defines one's personal identity within their family unit, but it also determines the identity and the direction of our societies. By recognizing this subtle and timeless conflict that affects every individual, along with every aspect of a society's culture and its institutions, it greatly simplifies one's understanding of the complex layers underlying the human social and cultural experience. Unfortunately, it is an area of study that has been woefully neglected and ignored by the academic community.

On the whole, these gender social patterns are not strictly male or female subcultures, but they do generally operate as such. Within every human being, there dwells a degree of both the masculine and feminine qualities. Together, they form the dualistic basis of our nature. Ultimately, the average human's disposition can be classified, much like a society, as either being predominately masculine or predominately feminine. And because of this sexual dichotomy, a male can be a part of a matri-culture just as easily as a female can be a part of a patri-culture, depending upon his or her inclination. Thus, the two opposing gender based subcultures have always comprised both genders. However as individuals, they do represent that particular gender's distinctive characteristics and qualities. Simply stated, there are males who possess predominant feminine qualities and there are females who possess predominant masculine qualities; which explains why, the stereotyping of any individual can be a completely misleading endeavor.[17]

By and large, the individuals within the patri-culture are masculine in nature and possess a high level of testosterone, which propels their sexual aggressiveness. Whether they are a male or a female, they are physically outgoing, assertive, introverted, independent, goal oriented, competitive, emotionally detached, rebellious, and analytical in their natural inclination. These individuals are a throwback to the days when our hunting societies were dependent upon their unique masculine characteristics. Even within modern times, they are attracted to same types of professions, hobbies, and entertainment. They seek out the same types of jobs; enjoy the same types of movies, music, and literature; wear the same types of clothes and enjoy the same types of sports. They even laugh at the same type of humor. Also, their political beliefs are similar as compared to their opposing matri-cultural brothers and sisters. However, their social, political, and economic supremacy would begin to slowly erode as our economies have progressed.[18]

In contrast, the individuals within a matri-culture are feminine in nature. As the females experience ovulation, menstruation, and eventually pregnancy, their hormone levels of estrogen, progesterone, and testosterone will rapidly rise and fall, which accounts for their mood changes. Within both genders, these individuals are essentially physically passive, extroverted, emotionally dependent, relationship orientated, cooperative, nurturing, and intuitive in their natural inclination. Throughout our past, they were victims to the whims of the more dominant patri-culture. Perceived as defenseless and thus inferior by the other subculture, their lives were filled with recurring abuse and never-ending exploitation. But within every aspect of society, the individuals within the matri-culture have made a tremendous impact. They may not have been as assertive or as physically aggressive as their patri-culture counterparts, but their contributions to our societies have nevertheless been just as immeasurable.[19]

These fundamental differences between the patri-culture and matri-culture have had a very significant and positive impact upon the evolution of our species. During times of natural disasters such as floods, fires, hurricanes, tornadoes, and earthquakes, along with any national emergency such as an economic depression, civil strife, or military conflict, these two subcultures will temporarily unify and then arise as one to deal with the challenges. By their very nature, they will combine their unique talents to work together for a common good, which is almost unheard of within the animal kingdom. Between the two of them, our societies have become extremely versatile in their adaptation to any form of natural or human calamity.

It is during these times of national emergencies and cultural unity that the distinction between the two subcultures becomes very vague. In the name of overcoming their societies' immediate peril, the individuals within the matri-culture will for the time being cease their conflict with those within the patri-culture and yield to their domination. But once they have overcome the emergency, the conflict will continue and sometimes even intensify.

Among the scientific community, it is believed by many individuals that our prehistoric societies were matriarchal in their social structure and relatively egalitarian until the advent of the agrarian revolution. And that we were basically a leaderless, stagnate, and disorganized group of free-spirited individuals. While enjoying the fruits of nature, we wandered from continent to continent wearing leaves, eating berries, and living in harmony. Regrettably, this belief is completely misguided and unsubstantiated by those who have chosen to ignore the tremendous impact of our economic evolution and the struggles our ancestors had to endure.[20]

Historically speaking, there have been a large number of predominately matriarchal societies where the matri-culture socially dominated. They were usually societies that were geographically out of harm's way of the more aggressive patriarchal societies. Although, these societies' were agrarian and somewhat egalitarian, the conflict between the two subcultures had been just as intense. Beginning in the family and stretching into every institution and human endeavor, this conflict of interests and priorities is an ever-ceasing struggle no matter which subculture predominates. For there exists within each individual, an element of chauvinistic behavior and resentment that continuously inflames the struggle. It has been so embedded within our psychic consciousness that many people are completely unaware of their innate bias (sexism) towards the individuals within the other subculture.[21]

From our very beginnings in the green forests of eastern Africa to our more recent nomadic past, the predominantly male patri-culture has dominated our societies, due to the males' ability to sustain our earlier economies. With exception of a few scattered matriarchal southern hunter-gatherer clans, the patri-culture would continue to dominate our societies for most of our past. However around 11,500 years ago, we began to farm the rich moist soil found along the world's great river systems. With the introduction of agriculture, the survival of our societies was no longer exclusively based upon the male's ability to hunt. Henceforth, the human economy would become based upon both the male's and the female's ability to cultivate the crops, raise the animals, and to produce the needed goods and services. Consequently as our agrarian economies became more successful, the matri-culture would begin to slowly exert itself. By becoming an even more an intricate part and contributor to our new farming economy, they would eventually become more influential throughout their respective cultures.[22]

It should be recognized that once a society becomes industrialized, the matri-culture will become the dominant social force. Finally able to compete on every economic and political level with the individuals within the patri-culture, their unique feminine characteristics will become the most valued and emulated. For unlike the nomadic and the agrarian societies, the masculine qualities exhibited by the individuals within the patri-culture will be discouraged and actually frowned upon by the surrounding cultural forces. Within a world dominated by technology, huge government bureaucracies, powerful corporations, and the mass media, which seeks to totally control our societies, the distinctive qualities exhibited by the individuals within the matri-culture are the best suited to succeed, where their natural inclination towards acquiescing, cooperating, and conforming are paramount.

The H. heidelbergensis were very complex social creatures who attempted to overcome the powers of nature by whatever means possible. Fundamentally, they were incestuous, cannibalistic, suspicious of strangers, and abundantly ruthless in their behaviors. But on a more positive note, they were also intensely devoted and caring parents, personally sacrificial and charitable, resourceful, and absolutely determined to adapt to their environment. In modern terms, they were extremely human in their habits, interpersonal relationships, and in their boundless desire to protect their own. Yet they were savages, attempting to survive in a savage land, where the probability of surviving was almost nonexistent for those species that couldn't adapt to the changing circumstances around them.

Chapter Six

The Middle Paleolithic Nomads
"Homo sapiens"

"Today, we stand with the brains of hunter-gatherers in our heads, looking out on a modern world made comfortable for some by the fruits of human inventiveness, and made miserable for others by the scandal of deprivation in the midst of plenty."

Richard E. Leakey (1944-)
Kenyan Paleoanthropologist and Conservationist

Ecological change is a universal constant, which can uniformly create life, sustain life, or terminate life. The evolutionary genesis of the hominid species as well as our own civilizations has been environmental change. For if our environment hadn't periodically turned colder and drier, the early australopithecines would never have eventually evolved into the Homo sapiens. As a species of the primate family, we haven't conquered our surroundings. Instead, we have learned to adapt to the crushing tides of change and overcome the competition around us.

At the onset of the Great Pleistocene Ice Age, our species began to experience several evolutionary leaps as a result of a large number of climatic changes brought about by the present Ice Age. For the next 2.5 million years, we progressively evolved from the H. habilis into the H. ergaster/erectus and then into the H. heidelbergensis. Subsequently, they would evolve into the H. sapiens and then finally into the present day Homo sapiens sapiens. However during this same period, our economy had also evolved from one of scavenging into nomadic hunting and then finally into farming and herding. These fantastic physical and economic leaps were the result of the numerous ebbs and flows of the glaciation periods, which induced our almost constant adaptation to the changing environment.[1]

Once the massive glaciers began to creep across the earth's surface, the nomads and animals of Eurasia were forced to migrate towards the equator. Even though the climate was milder and there was initially an abundance of vegetation, it wouldn't have taken a very long time before the northern nomads clashed with the southern hunter-gatherers (see chapter 4, page 57-58) in the central and southern regions. And since the competition for food was greatly intensified during these periods of extreme cold and over-crowding, the struggle for survival would have been extremely harsh, especially for the northern nomads.[2]

Needless to say, the southern hunter-gatherers had a tremendous advantage over the northern nomads in terms of surviving and finding new sources of food within their own environment. And although these unwelcomed northern nomads were highly mobile, organized, and armed to the teeth, their numbers were without question greatly reduced by the time the glaciers began to recede back to their poles. Therefore, it is of little wonder that our southern hunter-gathering ancestors would eventually evolve into an even more adaptable, imaginative, and healthier population, than their more northern nomadic cousins.

It has been estimated that approximately 200,000 years ago, the Homo sapiens (wise human) first appeared. While inhabiting the continents of Africa, Europe and Asia, they replaced the earlier hominid species that had dwelled in their particular regions. This occurred almost immediately after the Mindel-Riss interglacial period had ended and the Riss glaciation period was about to begin. It is believed that they either radiated out of Africa or that they were simultaneously springing up all around the globe.[3]

Today, the scientific community isn't unanimous on either theory. It is believed by many scientists that due to the H. ergaster/erectus continuous interbreeding, which created a balance between their genetic drift, gene flow, and the natural selection process, their development moved along in the same general direction. While maintaining their regional characteristics, it was these surviving varieties of H. ergaster/erectus that would directly evolve into our own H. sapiens. All across Eurasia and in Africa, they would suddenly appear, eventually forming our different ethnic groups and our diverse languages. The proponents of the "Multiregional" theory point to the fossil and genomic data, along with the continuity of the archaeological evidence as support for their hypothesis.[4]

However, the DNA evidence indicates that the H. sapiens evolved solely in Africa around 200,000 year ago. After migrating from Africa approximately 130,000 years ago, they replaced the earlier hominid populations, such as our own H. heidelbergensis and finally the Neanderthals. Despite several problems with this hypothesis, such as projecting a species actual population and their mutation rate, along with the DNA's unreliability as a molecular clock, the majority of the scientific community appears to support the "Out of Africa" theory, even though the archeological and linguistic evidence does not support it. But whatever the scenario, it really doesn't apply to our economic evolution. The nomadic H. sapiens were eventually able to claim the world as the lone survivors of the hominid family.[5]

Physically imposing and exceptionally shrewd, the H. sapiens displayed most of the physical characteristics of the modern day human. Standing between 5 feet 6 inches to 6 feet tall and weighing up to 190 pounds, their hands and feet were highly developed. Even though the H. sapiens' skeletons were lighter than their robust predecessors, they did have a curved spine and a narrow pelvis that effectively distributed their body weight for walking long distances. While possessing the largest brain (e.g.1350cc) of the hominid family, their high arched skulls were thin-walled with a vertical looking forehead. Also, their faces showed a much smaller brow ridge, a prominent chin and nose, and a small set of teeth that was surrounded by a less protruding jaw.[6]

At the beginning of the last glaciation period (Wurm-Weichselian) approximately 110,000 years ago, H. sapiens had already improved their ability to kill at a considerable distance by using an improved throwing spear, the dart-throwing atlatl, and quite possibly the first bows and arrows. As a group, the hunters could bring down any large animal by ambushing it and then shooting their darts or arrows into either its intestines or its hind legs. Then once the animal was wounded and crippled, they would surround it and then thrust their spears into its heart. Afterwards, it was just a matter of dividing the meat among themselves and then carrying it back to their camp.[7]

The H. sapiens' Aterian tool industry was comprised of an assortment of improved clipping tools that were fashioned in three different stages. Initially, the hunter clipped a stone into a long blade or into a rectangular shaped figure. Next, he would clip out a groove at one end, so as it could be tied to a wooden handle or pole. Then finally, he shaved the edges of the stone into a very sharp Levalloisian point. Compared to the previous tool industries (Oldowan, Acheulean, and Clactonian), their weaponry and tools were better constructed, sturdier, and more diversified. As a result, the average hunter could employ a wide variety of knives, scrapers, axes, arrows, spears, and cutting blades for many different purposes.[8]

The impact of making weapons and tools upon human civilizations runs much deeper than merely how societies have advanced through technological innovations. In fact, it had such a tremendous influence upon our perception of the world around us, and how we even perceive ourselves, that the repercussions of it can be felt even today. For when our ancestors began to produce weapons, clothing, tools, baskets, jewelry, and other items, they would inevitably look upon those items as their personal possessions, instead of as the communal property of the clan.

Envisioned and then produced by a person's own hands and imagination, these items could be kept, traded, or just given away as they became surpluses. But whatever their inclination, it was this introduction of handmade weapons, tools, and goods and their eventual surpluses that unknowingly created the concept of private property, which in turn would ultimately establish and maintain the individuals' social prominence within the clan. Later as we became farmers and herders, the concept of private property would be expanded to include animals, people (slaves), and land.

As Stone Age hunters, they were driven by their traditions, migration patterns, and hunger. They never farmed the land, raised an animal, or built a fence. They used tools made of stone, wood, and bone, while they huddled around their grass shelters. They made their clothes out of furs and watched their children play in the dirt among swarming insects. They lived under the sun, stars and the moon as they roamed the landscape in search of food. Always on the move and forever struggling against the elements, they stoically faced the dangers around them. While living day to day, their shortened lives were a mixture of temporary pleasures, frequent tragedies, and prolonged suffering. They were a determined people whose way of life would never ensure a large number of them. Even during the times of plenty, they cried over their dead, feared the unknown, and comforted the sick. They were a restless primitive people, who lived for the moment and never knew the joy of a promising future.

While wandering the earth's surface for almost 2 million years, our nomadic ancestors lived a lifestyle that demanded a high birth rate in order for them to have had any chance of survival. Undoubtedly, the females experienced an exceptionally high number of miscarriages, due to the rugged nature of constantly living in the outdoors and the physical demands placed upon them. And even when a child was born, the majority of them wouldn't have survived for very long. The lack of proper hygiene and prenatal care would have created a soaring mortality rate. Thus in response to the economic need to produce as many offspring as possible, our nomadic ancestors would slowly undergo several physical, biological, and cultural changes. In due course, these changes would include the enhancement of the males' already intensified biological sexual drive (libido) and a change in the females' physiological ability to bear more children.[9]

Within the broad spectrum of human evolution, the males with the strongest libidos had a distinct advantage over their less testosterone-driven males in reproducing more offspring. In the long run, this had a tremendous impact upon their roaming culture and our biological evolution as a whole. For generation after generation, the more dominant sexually inclined males were selectively breeding as a way to maintain their nomadic way of life. As a result, they were unknowingly creating a genetic pool of sexually hyper-active males, who could only satisfy their sexual needs by constantly relying upon their aggressive behavior. Hence, the male's intense sexual instinct (libido) was not only intensified even further, but it would also increase his aggressive drive towards his female counterpart as well. This intensification of the male's libido and his aggressive drive would metabolically make him an emotionally inclined introvert as compared to the average female. Since his most inner emotional and instinctual sexual needs were constantly being expressed and then fulfilled whenever he masturbated or copulated, there wasn't any motivation on his part to dwell on his feelings. His world was one of directing his personal and physical power towards a specific goal without pausing to evaluate how he felt about it.[10]

As the givers of human life, the males' primordial desire to copulate or to achieve ejaculations could be described as a form of biological addiction. Similar to a modern day drug addicts experiencing the sensation of having a monkey on their back, the young males would come to exhibit the same symptoms of physical irritation, frustration, obsessive behavior, and the loss of rational thought, whenever his reproductive drive wasn't being biologically satisfied. Subsequently, the males of our species have evolved into undeniably the most sexually obsessed and prolific creatures within the animal kingdom. They would find themselves an ardent prisoner to their own exhilarating and ever-present passion to spread their seed. It is a passion so overpowering that it can make an old man act like a childish fool and a young naïve one act like a reckless hero. Even today, if the average male isn't actively seeking out a sexual partner, he is usually fantasizing about it; unless of course, he has directed his sexual energy towards another goal. This form of habitual behavior doesn't make him morally weak, depraved, or even socially irresponsible and immature. Instead, it makes him quite human and deeply vulnerable.[11]

Contrary to modern scientific myth, which has not been substantiated in over 5,000 years of written history, the female of our species has evolved into a less sexually driven individual as compared to her male counterpart, thus exhibiting less physical aggression. However, the female of our species has always possessed the innate ability to sexually influence and guide the males towards their own particular goals, which could be called the understatement of the millennium.

As the producers of human life, the nomadic female of our species was primarily bred and raised to bear a large number of children, thus her physical adaptation came in the form of developing tremendously strong leg, buttocks, and back muscles in order to support her child bearing. Furthermore, the female's estrus would eventually disappear and be replaced by the much more fertile uterus as her pelvic bone became wider to ease the strain of child birth. Even though she possessed under-developed arm strength, she could still carry a heavy load on her back for long distances, while bearing a child in her womb. Unlike her primate predecessors, who gave birth to a single child every three or four years, she was soon able to produce children on a yearly basis. Literally pregnant throughout her brief existence, when she wasn't giving birth herself, she was usually assisting the other females in giving birth.[12]

For the average female, childbirth is an enormously terrifying, painful, wondrous, and unforgettable experience. It usually occurs about 38 weeks after conception. During that period, most pregnant women experience symptoms of nausea and vomiting, excessive fatigue, cravings for certain foods that are not normally sought out, and frequent urination particularly during the night. It is an extremely emotional and stressful time for the female. As her abdomen expands, her breasts will enlarge and become very tender. Then, she may experience back aches and even more discomfort as the movement of the fetus becomes stronger. Fortified by her desire to produce offspring, she will experience active labor pains that can last 8 hours or much longer, depending upon the frequency of her uterine contractions. Once her cervix has completely dilated, the baby's head will descend into the pelvic area (crowning) of the vaginal opening. As the female pushes or bears down, she will feel an intense burning or stinging sensation. Especially for first time mothers, the pain can be almost unbearable as the doctor or midwives assist the child out of the womb.[13]

Once the baby has been born and handed to its mother, her placenta (afterbirth) will separate from the wall of her uterus and then exit her womb. Then in a moment of supreme exhaustion and satisfaction, she will gaze into the eyes of her new born child and instantly realize that all the pain, discomfort, and anguish she had endured was in the end all worthwhile. Unfortunately, several complications could arise that will threaten both the child and its mother life, such as infections, perineum lacerations, and obstetric hemorrhaging. But as modern medicine and techniques have improved, these dangers aren't as prevalent as in the past. Overall, the females' ability to produce human life is a very fascinating, traumatic, and necessary event. It is an event that has ensured our species survival along with our genetic continuation. Moreover, it is a self-defining experience that she will always remember with ambivalence.[14]

This physical and biological adaptation to produce more children had a tremendous impact upon the females' maternal impulses. Comparable to the males' libido, they eventually developed an extremely forceful "mother instinct," rarely matched within the animal kingdom. Exceedingly possessive of their children and intensely protective of their dens, this inflamed instinct would make them extremely determined, adaptable, emotionally extroverted, resilient, and profoundly patient. Unlike the males' primary instinct to aggressively spread their seed and then impatiently move on to find another den, the females' maternal instinct is to organize and preserve the den, while nurturing her offspring into adulthood. Although, the two genders of our species evolved into completely different creatures in their sexual compulsions, self-perceptions, and priorities, their relationship would evolve into an indomitable partnership of one.[15]

Due to the extraordinary development of the males' inflamed libido and the females' profound sense of motherhood, our species has been able to historically overcome a succession of wars, famines, epidemics, natural disasters, and environmental changes. This ability to produce a large number of offspring, while surviving under the most extreme conditions, has been the foundation of our species success. Had we not possessed either one of our distinctive genders' characteristics, we would have remained a mere footnote in the passage of time.

In all likelihood, our species' homosexual inclination was handed down to us by our primate ancestors from the eastern forests of Africa. Within their small bands, the young males and females regularly engaged in such behavior, either as an alternative to mating or perhaps as a sexual preference. Primarily motivated by their sexual or reproductive drive, along with their emotional and biological inclination, it wasn't considered a social taboo among the food gatherers or among the scavengers as such. However as nomads, it was probably frowned upon, because of their need to sustain their clans' populations. Nonetheless, this sexual inclination towards homosexuality was eventually inherited by their agrarian descendants. By that time, homosexual behavior had become an intricate part of human societies. As a consequence, many of our ancient cultures embraced their presence, while many others wouldn't be so tolerant.[16]

Whether or not homosexuality has been genetically, biologically, or even psychologically inherited by an individual is still being hotly debated even today. Strictly speaking, if an individual is raised by homosexual parents to be attracted to his or she own gender, unless they have an inner attraction towards their own gender, they will remain attracted to the opposite sex. Apparently, there are many different reasons behind an individual's sexual inclination towards their own sex, a fact that will frustrate anyone attempting to study the subject. Yet one cannot deny that no matter what the culture or the period, it is quite common for the males and females of our species to experiment and to explore their own sexuality during their adolescent years. And in most incidences, this will include a degree of sexual experimentation with their own gender. As a result, it is during this period of adolescent experimentation that the individual will usually discover his or her sexual orientation.[17]

Unlike the nomadic female's compulsion for homosexuality, which was possibly derived from her "mother instinct," along with her biological and emotional attraction to her own gender, the male's homosexual impulse was most likely initially driven by his instinctual "libido." It is through this act of sexual gratification that a nomadic male was able to express and to fulfill his biological need to spread his seed, while emotionally satisfying his need to bond with those of his own sex. Within the realm of both hetero/homosexuality, those individuals that desire to dominate a relationship will intentionally seek out those individuals that want to be dominated and vice versa. This need to dominate or to be dominated by another individual was handed down to us from our primate ancestors. For better for worse, it was a very prominent aspect of being a highly socialized species, whose individual identity and status was derived from his or her hierarchal group.[18]

The human homosexual has always sought out an emotional and physical relationship with a partner who can best fulfill his or her biological and emotional needs. This type of human behavior has always been a part of our societies and it will continue to be so. As many scholars have come to recognize, there is no such thing as a homosexual, only homosexual behavior; thus asserting that they aren't any less human or any less normal than that of the average heterosexual.

Instinctively leery of outsiders, our nomadic ancestors were an extremely loyal group of people. Their survival depended upon working together within their close knit clans. Since their contact with the other the clans was extremely limited, their cultures remained stagnant without ever having the opportunity to exchange ideas or observe the many different ways of doing things. Individuality as we know it today didn't exist for them. They ate the same food, spoke the same crude language, wore the same type of clothing, prayed to the same spirits, and reacted to most situations in much the same manner. Due to their success as nomads, they began to imagine that they had been favored by the unknown powers around them. Thus within their mental framework, they had become the center of the universe and represented the heart and soul of what it meant to be a human.[19]

As a group, they undyingly believed in their own distinct relationship with the powers around them and the uniqueness of their way of life.

They worshipped the animals they hunted by performing rituals in their honor. They roamed the surrounding expanse as free as any creature on earth and were intelligent enough to recognize the wonder of it all. Standing at the apex of their food chain, they believed the sun and the stars evolved around them, because their way of life was the only path that appeased the spirit world. Immensely proud of their traditions and their way of life, they became very chauvinistic about their cultures. Viewing themselves as "The Chosen People," they would look upon any outsiders as being inferior, untrustworthy, and spiritually out of touch. Thus, the nomads would take their initial instinct of fearing any outsider and turn it into a full-blown cultural and spiritual prejudice.[20]

The Middle Paleolithic nomads sought immediate sensual gratification in the simple everyday pleasures of warmth, security, food, companionship, and sex. The sensation of the moment was more important to them than the memories of the past or the possibilities of the future. Living in the moment gave their lives a sense of meaning, while they struggled to scratch out a meager living. Personally dreaming of a better tomorrow or occasionally regretting a past deed didn't exist within their intellectual framework. To them, life was immediate, unforgiving, hostile, and completely centered around the moment. Thus, their hedonistic approach to living for today was not only a reaction to the dismal circumstances they faced, but it was also a reflection of their nomadic lifestyle and spiritual beliefs.

Spiritually, the nomads' beliefs were based upon a mixture of mysticism and animism. Within their day to day experiences, the world around them was deemed as contradictory, chaotic, whimsical, mysterious, and even magical. Everything around them seemed to possess its own unique life force, or rather a spirit all of its own. In order for them to gain an understanding or an explanation of a certain phenomenon, it was essential for them to study the spirit of the thing. Whether the phenomenon was an animal, a thunder storm, a rushing river, a tree, or the force of the wind, they believed it possessed a spirit, struggling within the same universe. As a result, the spirits weren't perceived as being centralized nor could they be rationalized. Instead, the nomad's world was perceived as an agglomeration of spirits that expressed themselves as the basic forces of nature; forces which were continuously colliding with each other.[21]

The concept of an omnipotent god or a group of gods wasn't a part of their belief system. They believed in their own individual power and the destiny of their group, which could only be obtained through the whims of the spirits. Unlike the deities of today, the nomads' spirits could only influence circumstances; they weren't expected to change them. Thus, their religious interpretation of the environmental phenomenon around them, or rather that of the spirits was directly tied to the economic concept of "plenty." Only after the spirits had provided them with plenty of animals to hunt, plenty of water to drink, and plenty of plants to eat could they proclaim themselves favored by the spirits. Within their mind-set, this favor could only be maintained by not violating their sacred taboos and thus alienating the spirits. Throughout their childhood, they were taught to behave in a certain matter as a way of ensuring their future good fortune.[22]

While living in a rootless economy that wasn't very conducive towards scientific thought, the early nomads could understand the concepts of cause and effect only on an elementary level. The killing of a helpless animal to provide food for their families, the clipping of a rock into a tool, and the making of a camp fire were all actions and results they could perceive and understand. But, they were incapable of understanding the phenomenon like the appearance of a comet, the rumbling of an earthquake, or the sudden illness among their own. In their minds, it must have something to do with the unseen mystical powers around them. While being naïve, superstitious, and suspicious of their surroundings, these powers would become a part of their spirit world, filled with mysterious omens, scared events, and random calamities. It was a world where magic prevailed over sweet reason, where fear triumphed over knowledge, and where hysteria succeeded over self-control. Therefore, the unexplainable events of their lives became the will of the spirits, which later would be translated by the agrarians as the will of god or the gods.[23]

The underlying basis behind the early nomadic religious beliefs was ignorance and fear. As they roamed the various parts of the earth, they feared almost everything and everyone. Within their short life spans and their limited experiences, these fears were based upon their profound ignorance of the world around them. They saw danger and mystery everywhere, because they were everywhere. Living from hand to mouth, they wandered the land never knowing what the powers of nature had in store for them. And because they didn't understand the basic physical laws around them, they lived an irrational terrified existence, an existence based upon superstition. While appeasing and worshipping the powers around them, such as the animals, the wind, the sun, and the earth, the state of their ignorance and fear would grow ever larger and deeper. In the end, it was this superstitious inclination that would form the spiritual basis of their cultures. Never really understanding the forces around them and always living in constant fear of them were the cornerstones of their spirituality.[24]

Paradoxically, this same superstitious reaction to our surroundings still exists today. Humans have always been extremely superstitious and we always will be. It is the very nature of our existence to fear the unknown, the future, and our inevitable mortal demise. It is also a part of our nature to react to that fear in some irrational manner. Within every modern religious institution, there is an element of the nomad's superstitious nature or inclination. It is an inclination that can propel an otherwise logical individual to endorse the occult, witchcraft, or an extreme political or religious position. The coming of science and technology may have reduced our state of ignorance, but the fear of our own fatality and that of the unknown is as old and as powerful as ever.

The H. sapiens, even in the best of times, lived an uncertain and brief existence. The harshness of their reality directly affected how they mentally approached the questions of life and death. For an individual wandering the wilderness, nature was a cluster of contradictions and mysteries, interrelated with a maze of unmistakable absolutes. It was a cosmic world filled with immediate pains and pleasures, frequent hopes and despairs, and overpowering joys and passionate fears. When the nomads searched for answers and directions to their future survival, they would intuitively look to their natural surroundings to provide them. Within the scope of their belief systems, every phenomenon such as the wind, the rain, the sun, and even the other animals had a spiritual significance. These natural wonders represented much more than just random occurrences. They represented the awesome powers of their surroundings. Powers to be worshipped and feared, but above all else, they were powers to be appeased through rituals.[25]

One of the first known rituals was the burying of their dead. Along with the Neanderthals, several H. sapiens' burial sites have been unearthed throughout Europe and the Middle East. The earliest undisputed human burial dates back approximately 100,000 years. Human skeletal remains stained with red ochre were discovered in the Skhul cave at Qafzeh, Israel. The body was also buried with an assortment of stone tools, sea shells, and animal bones, which could indicate they had developed a religious ideology that included the belief in an afterlife. Of course, no one really knows for sure the purpose behind the rituals. Several secular theories have been put forth by today's scientists, such as the clan showing respect for the dearly departed, providing family closure, hiding the odor of the corpse, or attempting to keep their remains away from scavengers have all been considered real possibilities. However, what this burial site did positively indicate was the presence of a shaman.[26]

In terms of their religious legacy, the nomads not only left behind their superstitious character and spiritual interpretation of events, but they also gave us the very foundation for modern religions. It wasn't a foundation based upon a written moral code or the heritage of erecting churches, temples, synagogues, and mosques. Instead, they gave us the significance of performing rituals, the necessity of implementing codes of behavior, and more importantly, the essential role of the religious leader, the shaman.[27]

Usually, the role of the shaman was a hereditary position handed down from father to son. However, the position could also be occupied by whoever demonstrated a talent for interpreting the whims of the spirits, which also included females. Depending upon the strength of their mystical powers, anyone could become a shaman, regardless of their age or gender. Of course, it is impossible to really know for sure when the shaman became an important part of the nomads' life. But when these spiritual leaders did emerge, their contributions to the evolution of human civilizations would be immense.[28]

In fact, it was these early shamans that would give the human race something far more important than mere rituals. For the first time in our existence, they attempted to explain the purpose of our lives and the meaning behind it all. And even though their metaphysical rationale was extremely primitive by today's standards, this was a very important part of our cultural development. Within the sometimes harsh and always unpredictable course of human events, it was this expression of purpose and meaning that provided us with an unshakable faith to carry on under the most extreme and adverse conditions. Whether a shaman was performing a ritual to control the powers of nature, counseling a disturbed individual, or just reassuring the group of better times ahead; their role as a clan's religious leader would become an indispensable part of the human experience. Rational or not, these holy men and women of the great outdoors would create a tradition of caring for the ill, counseling the anguished, assisting and protecting the helpless, and inspiring faith in others.[29]

Undoubtedly, our ancestors possessed an extremely high tolerance for physical pain and suffering. The nomadic economy demanded no less of its people. They didn't fear death, because it was all around them and a part of their daily experiences. For many suffering individuals, death was seen as a release from their miseries. On the whole, they were extremely resilient and hardy, but rarely healthy. Toughened by their daily struggles, they were usually hungry, exposed to the elements, and constantly filthy. In the winters months, they regularly suffered from pneumonia and frost bite. The older ones suffered terribly from rheumatism, loss of teeth, and intestinal diseases. Since they had a poor diet and lived in the open air, many of them experienced the anguish of arthritis or even blindness at an early age. A broken bone, scratches from a thorn, or a snake bite could lead to death in a matter of days. And yet, they continued to stoically endure and in many cases overcome the harshest injuries. This was made possible with the help of the clans' healer and the shaman.[30]

Initially, the parents took care of themselves and their children, whenever someone was injured or suddenly became ill. This arrangement lasted for a very long time and worked very well. However as the clans grew in size and complexity, the demand for a full time healer became paramount. Since the older alpha females had acted as midwives and were always caring for the health and welfare of their children and their mates, they invariably assumed the role of the clan healer. So long as the affliction was minor, the female healer was very successful in dealing with the everyday injuries of her patients. Over time, she would become an intricate asset and a person of immense status within the clans. However, she would have to momentarily step aside from her patient, if the injuries or the illnesses were beyond her skills. At that point, the shaman was expected to work his or her magic.

The nomadic shamans and healers didn't leave behind any huge libraries of medical data, nor did they develop any vaccines, surgical procedures, therapeutic technologies, or any preventive measures. But what they did leave behind was a ground-breaking medical legacy for later-day physicians. Within their many responsibilities, they were called upon to heal the sick, mend the injured, and ease the pain of the suffering. By establishing the role of doctor, they were probably the first individuals to apply the different types of herbal medicines, thermal cures, and simple surgeries to an individual's medical problem. As the pioneers in medicine, they would set the stage for the agrarian physicians to follow.[31]

Throughout their travels, the nomadic shamans and healers were astute enough to understand that broken bones had to be mended, bleeding had to be stopped, and that open wounds had to be closed or at least protected. Since they didn't understand the presence of germs or possessed the advantages of using clean bandages, they would apply either mud or a wad of moss to an open wound. Actually, this type of treatment worked fairly well for them. Once the mud or moss had dried and harden, it would adsorb the infectious bacteria and the secreting pus. Then as the wound would begin to heal and close, the application of mud or moss would be discontinued so that a scab could form.[32]

In all likelihood, the idea of using bandages came about for the purpose of keeping the mud or the moss on the wound until it could dry. While doing their daily chores, the application of a bandage would have helped ensure the proper healing of a wound. Meanwhile, the more advanced shaman and healers eventually learned to close a wound by searing it with a hot piece of wood or stone. It was a very painful process, but an effective one. Overall, each of these methods would prove quite effective in healing the majority of the minor wounds. However, if an individual's intestine or an artery happened to be pierced, the chances of their recovery were next to zero.[33]

In case of high fevers or some other serious symptoms, the clan's shaman was summoned to administer his medical herbs and potions. Familiar with the many beneficial effects of the various surrounding plants, they would mix a wide variety of plant roots, leaves, nuts, berries, or bark, minerals, pain-relieving plants, and even animal parts to create medicinal potions. Many of these potions did have therapeutic value in dealing with minor illnesses such as slight fevers, colds, or the aches and pains of everyday living. But it should be mentioned that the average nomad didn't live enough to acquire today's most dreaded health problems like heart disease, cancer, or high blood pressure. Many of their internal ailments weren't life threatening, unless of course, they were succumbing to a deadly disease or infection. More often than not, if the shaman's potions didn't help the patient, he or she would resort to magic in the form of charms, chants, and even prayers to the spirits. Later many of these rituals were performed while the shamans were under the influence of some hallucinogenic plant, which they believed gave them a greater insight and keener perception into the spirit world.[34]

The shamans came to possess a tremendous amount of psychological power over their people. As spiritual authority figures and healers, their exclusive relationship with the unknown powers around them created the perception that they possessed the ability to induce miracles. Through the use of chants, charms, and induced trances, they invoked the spirit world to come to their aid and perform a miracle. In times of need, they would call upon the wind to blow away a child's illness or summon the dark clouds in order to bring rain to a thirsty people.

Genuine or not, as a result of demonstrating their mystical powers, they spiritually dominated our early nomadic societies for possibly close to 100,000 years.[35]

In fact, their influence upon our religious institutions can be felt to this very day. Evangelistic ministers or priests, rabbis, pastors, and holy men from all over the world will use charms, chants, and prayers to invoke their deities blessing to miraculously cure one of their ailing flock. This usually occurs only after modern science has given up any hope for curing the individual. Undoubtedly, this calling out to god or gods for assistance is indicative of how deeply embedded the old shamans' beliefs and methods had been instilled within our cultures.

Over the span of time, the nomads also gave their future generations something much more important to the present theologies than just ceremonies or sermons. In a very direct way, they gave us the deities (spirits) to protect us, guide us, and to show us the way to salvation. It wasn't by happenstance that the early agrarian societies established polytheism (numerous gods) as their initial religion. These gods didn't just suddenly appear to their agrarian spiritual leaders as deities to be worshipped. They were an extension of the spirits that the nomads had worshipped. It was only later that these nomadic spirits were given human form (anthropomorphic) and renamed as gods by the clergies of the agrarian religious institutions.[36]

Since the acts of incest and pedophilia provoke such strong emotions within today's general public, it should be remembered that these behaviors are not a unique phenomenon. They didn't just suddenly appear in our present time, due to the decline in our society's moral standards. As a matter of fact, these types of abhorrent behaviors have been a part of human existence long before we ever became nomads. For the last 5 million years of our evolution, they have become in all likelihood an unwelcomed instinctual part of our species. Rightfully viewed as socially and morally outrageous crimes of society, contemporary governments have enacted strict laws to eliminate such behaviors, especially where children have been involved. Yet unfortunately, these behaviors still persist to this day in almost every society, because they have been and will continue to be a part of our primordial psyche.[37]

Today, a number of scholars have theorized that the horrors of warfare and the strategic and tactical concepts behind it are uniquely human inventions; and that until our species came upon the scene, the earth was in complete harmony as the surrounding animals peacefully lived together amid the plush green vegetation and gleaming skies. Actually, nothing could be further from the truth.

Long before our nomadic ancestors came into existence, warfare was being continuously waged within the animal kingdom. Between the many different species of mammals, fish, insects, and birds, they have been conducting a continuous form of guerrilla war. The outcome has always been predicated upon which species was the swiftest, sneakiest, strongest, and the most numerous. And when the carnivores weren't locked in a territorial struggle with each other, they were usually attempting to catch and then devour some unfortunate animal that had happened to be at the wrong place at the time. Individually and as a group, the surrounding animals struggle for survival is every bit as savage and ruthless as human warfare. The level of nature's viciousness knows no bounds nor does it spare the young, the old, or the helpless. Thus, we weren't the creators of war nor were we the first species to kill our own. The animals and the other life forms before us have that distinction. While institutionalizing the brutality of it all, we just expanded the conflict by introducing a wider range of weaponry and a higher level of organization.[38]

Whether the H. sapiens lived in the cold northern steppes or the southern forests and coastlines of Eurasia, they struggled against each other with the objective of gaining, retaining, or enlarging their territories. It was a reason the whole clan could understand and enthusiastically embrace. Warfare in and of itself would become an important aspect of their culture. Life without it was unthinkable in a world that favored those who were prepared to arm themselves and seize the fruits of their surroundings. This had nothing to do with blood lust or the inherent human desire for aggression. Rather, it was a cultural choice on the part of the clans to economically secure the richest territories by sustaining a patriarchal society for the purpose of continuously waging war against both man and animal. The stakes were incredibly high amid a sea of unceasing competition and unpredictable climatic changes. But, the rewards were even greater for the men and women who wanted to prosper. Thus, the very nature of embracing a roaming economy would force the clans to be in a constant state of conflict. Whether they liked it or not, they had to defend their place under the sun against all would-be competitors. The prosperity of the hunt and that of their clans would dictate no less.[39]

In a sense, the nomads didn't own their territories any more than they could own the sky or the trees. But possession was nine tenths of the law. Those clans that occupied an area, they temporarily claimed as their own, until they either moved to greener pastures or were driven away by a more powerful clan. Contrary to the agrarian farmers who would fight to the death for their land, our roaming ancestors cherished and revered certain places, but they never perceived them as things to own or even to die over. Within their magical world of spirits and incomprehensible forces, the land was endless and a source of life that gave meaning and substance to their existence. It was a gift from the spirits that didn't belong to anybody. Within their mind-set, the idea of fighting and dying in great numbers over a piece of land was beyond their understanding. Thus, nomadic warfare was actually a series of small skirmishes, where the loser was always free to run away to fight another day.[40]

Due to the hunters' need to find game and reproduce as many offspring as possible, nomadic warfare was restricted in scope and considerably less deadly than today's conflicts. Usually fought during the spring and summer months, their tactics were based upon gradually killing off or scaring away another clan's warriors. They didn't fight wars of extermination, because they couldn't afford to lose very many hunters in the process. Thus, the H. sapiens' intent was to slowly enlarge their territories by driving away their less powerful neighbors through the slow elimination of their hunters. Later, wars of extermination probably did occur, when the competition for food with the Neanderthals had greatly intensified during the last glaciation (Wurm-Weichselian) period.[41]

When the weather permitted it, our ancestors would conduct raids into their enemy's territories. The raids were usually carried out by a war party, which consisted of a small number of warriors. The main purpose behind the raids was to secretly penetrate an enemy's peripheral territory and ambush a few of their hunters. Much like their primate ancestors before them, their basic strategy was to slowly and methodically kill or maim as many of the enemy's hunters as possible, so that they would eventually be unable to feed their clan or defend their territory. To achieve this goal, the raiders employed a wide variety of tactics such as deceptions, diversions, decoys, and ambushes in order to render the other clans' defenseless. Needless to say, it was a very drawn-out type of warfare. But if the raiders were successful in their mission, they could significantly enlarge their territory.[42]

Whenever a war party happened to suddenly and unexpectedly encounter another clan's group of warriors, it had become customary from their ancient past to initiate a form of ceremonial demonstration. At the moment of confrontation, it must have been a terrifying spectacle for them to have beheld. Suddenly, the individuals within each group would begin to jump up and down, while they screamed at the top of their lungs and waved their crude weapons up in the air. Among the snarling anger and the dreadful fear, they attempted to intimidate each other through their frightful appearance and ferocious looking behavior. Ordinarily, the group that could scream the loudest, jump the highest, and appear the fiercest could in many instances achieve a bloodless victory against a less determined foe.[43]

If a group of warriors outnumbered their opponents, these boisterous demonstrations usually produced the desired results. In a moment of clarity, the smaller group would hesitate for a minute and then begin to slowly back away. Occasionally, a few of them would throw their spears at the larger war party as they retreated; but in general, they weren't inclined to stand and fight. Militarily, they specialized in hit and run tactics against a numerically inferior foe. The whole concept of a clan standing their ground and endangering their families' survival by possibly losing most of their bread-winners in a single engagement was beyond their imagination. They viewed warfare as a sort of game to be waged only on their own terms, where their success was assured.

Unfortunately as the last glaciation (Wurm-Weichselian) period began pushing the Neanderthals out of northern Eurasia approximately 100,000 years ago, warfare would take on a whole new dimension in its ruthlessness and ferocity.[44]

Chapter Seven
The Upper Paleolithic Nomads
"Homo sapiens sapiens"

"To genetic evolution, the human lineage has added the parallel track of cultural evolution."

Edward O. Wilson (1929-)
American Biologist

During the ebb and flow of the present Ice Age, the lives of the H. sapiens were disrupted by several periods of expanding and receding glaciers that would alter their migration patterns. In the northern regions, the restless nomads continued to follow and hunt the massive herds of animals, wherever they might wander, while the southern hunter-gatherers remained in their isolated sanctuaries. Even though their day to day existence was a struggle for survival, they were still able to reproduce enough offspring so as to ensure their way of life. Then suddenly around 45,000 years ago, as the polar glaciers were expanding during the middle of the (Wurm-Weichselian) glaciation period, something astonishingly occurred to our species that modern scientists and scholars have continued to debate to this very day.

Coinciding with the arrival of the Homo sapiens sapiens and the appearance of our different ethnic/racial groups, a cultural revolution seems to have taken place in many parts of the world. Referred to as the Great Leap Forward, it was unlike anything we had ever experienced before. For the first time, our species began to exhibit a truly human culture. Besides making colorful beaded jewelry, bracelets, necklaces, toys, and pendants, they also enjoyed the sounds of the first known musical instrument, the simple lute, which indicates the ability to sing. Decorated on the walls of their caves were darken images of the surrounding animals that exhibited a newfound intuitive creativeness. They also began to make bone and ivory sculptures in the form of three dimensional figurines. They weaved fabrics into clothing, created oil lamps, and constructed semi-permanent shelters out of mammoth bones and tusks that were then covered with branches and animal hides. Our ancestors even constructed boats and made their way to Australia and the South Pacific islands. And finally, they had developed the Aurignacian tool industry, which produced a wide variety of specialized tools and weaponry that would help bring about the concept of specialized labor.[1]

Without question, this little known period of human advancement ranks right up there in importance with the domestication of plants and animals and the Industrial Revolution. Only on a very few occasions has our species experienced such influential periods, where we have taken such a significant step forward.

Presently, there are several different theories for this remarkable evolutionary jump. One theory states that the Great Leap Forward suddenly occurred around 40,000 to 50,000 year ago as a result of a genetic mutation and a reorganization of our brain. As a theory, it is dubious at best, because it ignores over 3 million years of continuous hominid development. A second and more convincing theory holds that through the gradual accumulation of our knowledge and cultural development over the last several hundred thousand of years, we eventually acquired many modern human behaviors as a consequence of our self-perpetuating evolutionary loops. As a result, our species had finally reached a significant level of evolutionary advancement in our reasoning power, language efficiency, and in our organizational skills to the point where our cultural development was able to make a giant step forward. In other words, it was a cultural leap that was going to happen sooner rather than later.[2]

Around 45,000 years ago, a wide variety of different H. s. sapiens' cultures were flourishing within every unimaginable climate. It was also during this time that we evolved into our distinctively different ethnic (racial) groups. Now, it isn't entirely known why this phenomenon occurred. But within today's scientific and academic communities, there isn't a more volatile subject then that of our ethnic differences. It is a subject that has become so politicalized, and for some very good reasons, that there is very little consensus among the academic communities as to what are our ethnic differences or even if they even do exist. Ironically, the average person in almost every part of the world believes those ethnic differences do exist and whatever the present day genetic or biological findings indicate, they will continue to do so.

Beginning in the 19th century, the scientists assumed that our species was comprised of three different and identifiable ethnic groups, which were designated as the Caucasian, Mongoloid, and the Negroid races. The scientists reasoned that since the earth's changing environment was the primary factor behind our species amazing evolution, it was only logical to them that it was also the primary factor behind the development of these ethnic groups.

It was deduced by these early scientists that since the Europeans exhibited the physical characteristics of pale skin, wavy hair, small nasal passages, thin lips, hollow bones, and light colored eyes; that they must have evolved in the extremely cold climate of northern Eurasia. In their minds, these types of physical characteristics couldn't have developed in any other environment. Then practically possessing the opposite physical characteristics of the Europeans, the Africans must have evolved from an extremely arid, hot desert climate. Their unique curly head and body hair, dark colored skin, steatopygia (enlarged buttocks), wide nasal passages, thick bones, and dark tinted eyes are indicative of a group of people who evolved from a severely dry and very hot environment. And lastly, the Asians with their olive colored skin, straight hair, eyelid (epicanthal) folds, very little body hair, short in stature, and broad faces must have dwelled in a moderately hot and humid climate, where the conditions weren't nearly as extreme as for those living in the deserts or in the cold northern regions.[3]

Of course, this is an oversimplification. But, it should be noted that their ethnic criteria wasn't based upon the color of a race's skin, but rather upon an ethnic group's facial and body features, bone density, and hair characteristics. Within this earlier system of classification, the aborigines of Australia and the Indians of India had been classified as Caucasian.

Then sometime during the middle of the 20th century, scientists were beginning to conclude that there are many different ethnic groups of people and not just the previous three. Since there are numerous ethnic sub-groups within each of the three major ethnic groups of people, it was believed that they should also be defined as a separate race unto themselves. And yet, many others scientists noted with a degree of confidence that these numerous sub-groups are actually an offshoot of their primary ethnic group and therefore not truly a separate race of people.[4]

Today, many geneticists and biologists have proclaimed that there is only one race of people, the human race. And that our ethnic differences are really a social construct, or rather a social misperception that was established during the Europeans' colonial period. And that any discussion of ethnic grouping is an extension of our bias traditions and perceptions.[5]

Then, there is another group of modern scientists and scholars who believe we do possess several biological differences, which determines our ethnic differences. They have asserted that these differences were initially instigated by several factors. These factors include our sexual selection practices within a particular group, the natural selection process, the genetic diversity of an isolated group, and the environmental influences upon the group that lived in a particular region. But whatever the value of these arguments, which coincidently has nothing to do with our economic evolution, our species has evolved into an astonishing variety of colors, sizes, shapes, and physical characteristics, which has undoubtedly contributed to our uniqueness and vitality.[6]

After enduring a long period of time in isolation and surviving in the most adverse conditions, the various groups of roaming H. s. sapiens had begun to develop their own cultural traits. Rich in traditions, diverse in lifestyles, and acclimated to a particular environment, the development of our different ethnic groups has tremendously strengthened and added a new dimension to our species. Without a doubt, it was a monumental event in our evolution. For the first time, our species would begin to blossom and multiply into a human tree of cultural variety and distinctiveness that would ultimately enlarge and enrich the definition of the human race. And due to our different ethnic groups and cultural flexibilities, our species have become even more versatile in adapting to any future environmental changes.[7]

Even though the different ethnic groups have strengthened our species by their amazing diversification; it has also revealed the darker side to our nature. Based upon our ancient innate fear and mistrust of strangers and the willingness to exploit those strangers, our ethnic prejudices would appear soon after we had first begun to come into contact with the each other. Regrettably, this type of behavior was even more amplified by the economic consequence of limited resources versus the unrelenting human demand and competition for those resources. Unfortunately, those ethnic groups that weren't able to defend their precious resources were generally viewed as being inferior and thus undeserving. Coincidently, it was during this same period that the enslavement of other human beings would begin to raise its ugly head.[8]

One of the less admirable aspects of economic competition is that there is a human inclination to discriminate against the other competitors. Whether or not an individual belongs to a different race, gender, religion, nationality, sexual preference, or financial standing, we have always showed a prejudice against anyone whom we deem as a threat to our economic welfare and cultural lifestyle. Unfortunately, it has been so embedded within our psychic that if we are unable to discriminate against one group of individuals, due to the society's laws or cultural taboos (e.g. racism, sexism, or religious beliefs), then we will inevitably resort to discriminating against some other type of group. Generally speaking, a large number of modern industrialized people believe that they are bias free in their attitudes. However, this is usually not the case. Since our individual differences are so great and the economic competition is so intense, it isn't very difficult for an individual to find someone to loathe and to exclude from his or her inner circle. This sort of bias and fearful behavior is but an extension from our days as nomads. Yet much like our males' inflamed sexual instinct to reproduce in large numbers, the nomadic economy would take our prejudicial behaviors to new heights.[9]

In a pure economic sense, one of the main reasons the nomadic economy was so highly successful in overcoming the dramatic climatic changes of the present Ice Age was the development of surplus labor in the form of slavery. Due to our ancestors' short life spans and a high mortality rate among their infants, an extra pair of hands was always needed to assist in their survival. By and large, the slaves provided the needed help to ensure the emergence of specialized labor. Their presence allowed the clan members to concentrate their own efforts on developing and improving the needed skills to make everything from weapons, tools, shelters, and winter clothing to jewelry. In fact, the slave themselves would become so important to the nomads that they would eventually alter the clans' military strategies for the sole purpose of capturing them.[10]

In return for food, shelter, and protection, the slaves were required to perform any number of menial tasks, such as collecting firewood and water, gathering fruits, seeds, roots, or plants, preparing the pelts for clothing, and erecting temporary shelters. While they were busy performing these simple tasks, the clan's hunters were free to spend more time doing what they did best, making weapons, hunting for food, and protecting their territory. But, it was as a beast of burden that these slaves would become truly indispensable. By carrying the ever-larger and heavier loads of essential items from hunting ground to hunting ground, they enabled our hunting ancestors to become even more efficent.[11]

For the average slave, the dream of escaping back to one's own clan or species was in all likelihood not a very realistic expectation. Many of the clans' territories were so vast or isolated that the escapees would have either died of thirst or been eaten by predators long before they had reached familiar territory. Similar to the later-day Egyptian, Greek and Roman slaves, the majority of the slaves would have eventually acknowledged their bleak situation. Surrounded by strangers in a strange land with very little hope of obtaining their freedom, they would have had no choice but to accept their lower social status. And as long as they contributed something to the success of the clan, they could expect a share of the hunters' bounty and the many benefits of living within a secure camp. But when a slave was considered useless or too rebellious or too old, he or she could find themselves being used as bait to help ambush a particularly nasty predator.[12]

Overall, the enslavement of humans created a source of wealth for the owners. Once they had been captured at a very early age, the slaves could be trained and then utilized as laborers or possibly traded away to another clan as a valuable commodity. Eventually handed down to our agrarian forefathers, slavery would become such a powerful institution that it helped form and sustain many of the world's earliest empires. And incredibly, it still exists to this day in the more remote regions of the world. Like it or not, the institution of slavery in early times would become a very important economic aspect to our continued survival and to the later-day agrarians' prosperity.[13]

It should be noted that the many of these captured slaves were in all likelihood the children of Neanderthals. This would explain the very small genetic difference (.3%) between us and how we were in position to interbreed with them. However as a separate and competing species, the idea that as different species we lived in harmony together by respecting each other's differences is highly unlikely. In the middle of the (Wurm-Weichselian) glaciation period, approximately 45,000 years ago, the walls of the glacier ice were pushing the Neanderthals southward across Eurasia into the H. s. sapiens' hunting grounds. From the first moment of contact, they undoubtedly looked upon each other as a life-threating competitor. Due to the slow disappearance of the larger animals (megafauna) by their over-hunting, changes in the climate, and maybe even diseases, the competition between them would have only intensified. Yet unlike our ancestors, the Neanderthals wouldn't have kept any slaves. As cannibals, their captives were viewed as just another source of food. This could explain their abrupt extinction around 30,000 to 35,000 years ago. By this time, our ancestors had probably already began making cannibalism a taboo, whereupon they would have viewed the Neanderthals with overwhelming rage and repulsion.[14]

The Upper Paleolithic humans were mobile, competitive, and increasingly productive in crafting their wares. They didn't just begin trading (bartering) out of some mysterious motivation or out of mere accident. They began trading with the appearance of surpluses and the increase demand for them. Surpluses such as weapons, tools, clothes, footwear, toys, jewelry, baskets, musical instruments, food, slaves, and even personal services such as tattooing and skin piercing were all exchanged in order to fulfill an individual's needs. Now whether these marketplaces existed between the different types of hominids (e.g. H. s. neanderthalensis and H. ergaster/erectus) is unlikely, but they certainly must have existed between the H. s. sapiens' families within the clans and ultimately between the wandering clans themselves. It was a system of trading that would benefit everyone, so long as they had something to trade. In the fullness of time, these temporary marketplaces would become quite popular and even essential to their way of life.[15]

Trading between the various clans wasn't a planned, organized affair, but it undoubtedly did occur whenever the opportunity arose. And undoubtedly, the success of their transactions only led to more transactions, thus inspiring the clans' skilled laborers to produce even more goods. Overall what made this bartering system work so well was that the value of each item was based upon its level of supply and demand. As a result, the medium of exchange was inherently balanced between what was valued and available and what was not. Moreover, these exchanges were the natural consequence of the clan's desire to acquire essential or nonessential items, depending upon an individual's wants and needs. The idea of an individual intentionally acquiring wealth for the sake of wealth itself wouldn't come about until after we had begun to farm the soil.[16]

Throughout their scattered clans, our nomadic ancestors established the first marketplace. It was based upon an individual's self-reliance, initiative, imagination, and hard work. In their attempt to obtain unavailable items through the simple act of trading, those individuals who could produce the most desirable goods and provide the most satisfying services would all be rewarded for their efforts. But even more importantly, these temporary marketplaces would eventually instigate the first political and economic alliances between the trading clans. Once they had gotten to know and trust each other during these trading sessions, it was just a matter of time before they would begin to unite and form actual tribes. Although, the average person was leery of strangers and highly ethnocentric, the benefits of combining their clans would have far outweighed their wish to remain culturally excluded and economically isolated.[17]

It isn't certain when the institution of marriage first appeared, but many scientists and scholars believe it possibly began as a ritual in the confirming the alliances between the clans for the purpose of forming a tribe. By jointing in matrimony the leaders and the daughters of the separate clans, they were able to consecrate the union of the tribe by establishing blood ties between them, thus ensuring every ones' loyalty and devotion to the tribe as a whole. Since the act of pair-bonding had already existed for quite a long time, the ritual of marriage eventually began to slowly expand into the rest of the clan as a means of legitimizing their relationships.[18]

Still and all many scientists and scholars have theorized that marriage was a way of signifying a man's ownership of a woman for the purpose of curtailing the other males' competition for her services. In this fashion, the tribe's harmony and unity could have been maintained between the males, while at the same time securing the females' place within her hierarchy. It has also been theorized that it began as a way to validate the former pair-bonding roles of man and wife; whereupon clarifying and confirming the man's role as the provider and the safe keeper of the family, along with the woman's role as the man's child bearer and the family's caretaker. But whatever the initial reasons, the further bonding of man and woman into a sanctified family unit would inevitably strengthen our ties and ensure our species' success.[19]

In an effort to consolidate their power, establish civil harmony, and to protect themselves from outside aggressors, they slowly began unifying their clans into tribes by utilizing their social hierarchy as a form of chain of command. Since the females followed the males and the males followed the clan leaders, the tribal system was eventually instituted by the consent of the clan leaders out of economic necessity. In their mind-set, a clan could either remain isolated and vulnerable to the surrounding competition or they could band together with another clan and become even more powerful and secure in their undertakings. For the smaller clans, it was basically a choice of either increasing their chances of survival through their amalgamation or they could continue to exist on the edge of extinction. As a result, the clans that unified and formed the biggest and the most organized tribes would have a distinct economic advantage over the others. Of course, it will never be known for sure when this consolidation into tribes actually occurred. However, it probably happened during the period of our Great Leap Forward.[20]

Undeniably, it was a huge turning point in our evolution. For the first time, we began to seriously organize ourselves by establishing a tribal authority, based upon a system of tribal laws. It was a system that would ultimately weld the various clans together into a sizable mobile force that would leave behind an unforgettable legacy for our future governments to follow.

Almost overnight, these newly formed tribes were able to secure a better life for their offspring. By unifying their clans, they instantly increased their economic resources, expanded the size of their territories, and enlarged their genetic pool. As a matter of fact, this amalgamation of the clans and the forming of a governing authority was so beneficial to our species' prosperity that we would continue the process throughout the rest of our history. The eventual appearances of villages, kingdoms, empires, and even that of the modern day nation states are all prime examples of our species' continuous desire to combine our resources for the purposes of increasing our productivity and thus ensuring our prosperity and security.[21]

As an extension of the authority role performed by the scavenging alpha males and the leaders of the nomadic clans, a large number of the tribes continued to employ a single leader system. This governmental structure was based upon the leader's personal authority and the overriding confidence that the tribe had in him. Usually, he was a rare individual who was capable of leading his people during the harshest of times. As the leader or rather the chieftain, he was not only physically superior to those around him, but he was also a man of keen perception. In direct contrast with the concept of an omnipotent dictator, the tribe's customs and traditions would direct and mold the chieftains every option. On a day to day basis, he could rule as he deemed fit, but only under a set of specific cultural and social guidelines. Much like the kings and queens of the European Middle Ages, their authority was only as great as the men and women willing to serve under them. Thus, he wasn't the all-powerful tyrant envisioned by many people of today.[22]

Among the newly formed tribes, it would become customary for the fallen chieftain's oldest male descendant to take his place. This right of first succession was a logical outgrowth of the tribes' need to have stability. As the leader's direct descendants, the male heirs would have acquired a measure of political experience in their own right. Since they had been born of the same blood and lived under the authority figure's tutorage, the other members of the tribe came to look upon the male descendants as the best-prepared individuals for the awesome responsibilities of leadership. But when the leader's male descendants weren't old enough or incapable of fulfilling the role, another dominant individual and his family could rise to challenge their right to rule. These power struggles between the different clans within the tribe could occur at any time. Even though they had unified, the clans still maintained their individual identities. Thus, the average tribe could possess several potential ruling families, vying for the top spot.[23]

The single leader structure had not only created the right of first succession, but it also created the very concept of family rule. Recognized as the tribe's authority figure, the chieftain would establish the cultural and political precedent for his family members to rule in his absence, either while he was away on a hunting excursion or incapacitated due to illness. It was a precedent founded and sustained by the tribe's need to have someone in command at all times. As direct relatives of the chieftain, they were able to develop their own power bases within the tribe, which would form a kind of roaming monarchy. This establishment of his family's authority was ultimately formed by the consent of the heads of the various clans, but it was also formed by the chieftain's dominant personality. As a group, the tribe would reap the economic benefits behind the continuous authority and organization brought about by a single leader and his line of descendants.[24]

By this time, many of the southern hunter-gatherer tribes were primarily matriarchal in their social structure (see chapter 4, page 57-58), whereas their family lineage was remembered and recognized through the female members. Unlike their northern nomadic cousins, the females had a profound influence over any important decisions concerning the tribe that didn't apply to defending their territory. Once a tribe had established its own territory, their movements were restricted within that territory. Thus, their contact with the other tribes was extremely limited, which lessened the need for the males to act as warriors. And since they didn't follow the herds and there were many other sources of available food, the males' economic prerogative to rule was greatly diminished. However, it was during the times of conflict between the tribes that the males would become solely responsible for their survival.

Since it was the southern hunter-gatherers that formed the earliest agrarian societies along the great river systems, they would retain their governing bodies that had worked so well for them in the past. The governing structure that consisted of a sole leader with his eldest son having the right of first succession would later directly lead to the rise of the agrarian royal families. By following the past tribal precedents, these agrarian kings and queens would rule their realms under the same restrictions and privileges as that of the earlier chieftains. Politically limited in their authority and hampered by the laws and customs of the land, these monarchs were still able to amass enormous power, so long as they had the support of those around them, especially those of their religious leaders.[25]

Contrary to popular belief, the concept of a checks and balances within a governmental system didn't begin in modern times. The concept is as old as the nomads themselves. Long before the Greek philosophers began to write about the ethics of government and the rulers responsibilities to the people, the early nomads had already learned to divide the governing authority within their societies. This division of power was an idea born from harsh experience and the fruits of practicality. For instance, sometimes a tribal chieftain and his dominating family could be very oppressive and ineffectual as rulers. As a result, the clan leaders were the only individuals within the tribe that were powerful enough to challenge their right to rule. In many incidents, this situation could lead to a mini-civil war within the tribe, since the ruling family would rarely give up their political power without a struggle. Consequently, a large number of nomadic tribes would establish a duel-leader system as a counter-balance to the ineffectual and unacceptable leadership of a sole leader and his family.[26]

This duel-leader system (diarchy) was based upon dividing the leadership responsibilities of the tribe between a civil chieftain (shaman) and a tribal chieftain. Even though these two individuals represented two completely different spheres of authority, they were expected to coordinate their efforts as a unified whole. In simple terms, the tribal chieftain managed the day-to-day decisions of finding game, securing their territory, or conducting a war against another tribe. While at the same time, the civil chieftain would manage the tribe's domestic and spiritual affairs. As many tribes soon discovered, there were several advantages to having two rulers instead of just one. In the larger tribes, the responsibilities of leadership were just too vast for one individual to completely manage.[27]

Overall, the role of the civil chieftain was customarily, but not always, filled by the tribal shaman. As an established spiritual leader, he was already responsible for handling the domestic affairs and interpreting the spirit world through his many rituals and public orations (sermons). Admired for his wisdom, knowledge, and spiritual guidance, he was usually an older individual whose powers of magic and insight were held in awe by everyone. In terms of dealing with the complicated issues of domestic affairs, his services were invaluable to sustaining tribal harmony. Spiritually and socially, he was the glue that kept them together. Within any given day, he was expected to function as the tribe's judge, psychologist, family counselor, doctor, minister, and fortune teller.[28]

Unlike the tribal chieftain, the civil chieftain wasn't appointed or elected to his or her post by the heads of the clans. Trained by the father or the mother before them, the position was normally handed down to the offspring. Thus, anyone could become a civil chieftain, but only after he or she had successfully demonstrated their power in manipulating the spirit world. As a political counter-balance to the usually younger and sometimes overly emotional tribal chieftain, the civil chieftain was expected to exercise caution and reason during times of crisis. To his or her people, the civil chieftain represented the characteristics of patience, wisdom, and forethought.[29]

As for the tribal chieftain, he was usually a younger man of physical statue that stood head and shoulders above everyone else. When it came to demonstrating his physical qualities, he could dominate everyone around him. In relationship to his responsibilities, the chieftain's domain was in the realm of providing food and safety for his tribe. But when he wasn't out directing a hunting excursion or securing the tribe's territory, his powers were extremely limited by the observance of tribal customs and traditions. Around the campsite, he didn't possess the authority to order his people about against their will, unless they so desired it. But during the hunting season or during the time of war, he was expected to command, while the others were expected to follow. To his people, the chieftain represented the characteristics of aggressiveness, strength, bravery, and self-confidence.[30]

Usually, the tribal chieftain was more powerful and influential than the civil chieftain. Yet much of his power was based upon the success of the tribe. If he happened to fail in finding the wandering herds or in successfully defending the tribe, someone else could step forward and replace him. As for the civil chieftain (shaman), his position of authority was usually more secure than that of the tribal chieftain. During times of misfortune, he could always blame his failures upon someone else by declaring that an individual within the tribe had committed some sort of taboo, which had angered the spirits. Under this dual governing system, the emergence of the civil chieftain and the important social roles that he or she fulfilled would in due course forge a unique relationship between them and the tribal chieftain. For all intents and purposes, the tribal chieftain and his family would need the civil chieftain to approve and legitimatize their rule, while the civil chieftain required their legal protection and support in maintaining his or her position as the civil and religious leader. As a result, the tribal chieftain and the civil chieftain were forced to mutually support each other, whether they liked each other or not.[31]

Historically speaking, the royal monarchies and the religious establishments of the later-day agrarian societies just didn't suddenly appear once we had begun to domesticate the plants and animals. They were an extension of the power structures that had already been formed by the nomads. And incredibly, the transition was a relatively smooth one. The roles of the tribal leader and that of the civil chieftain had already been established and functioning well for an untold number of millenniums. Together with their religious leaders, the kings and queens of ancient Babylon, Egypt, Greece, and the more recent Buckingham Palace would undeniably owe their places of ascendancy to the scrawny, ill-kept nomadic aristocrats of the past.[32]

And finally, there was the council form of government. This type of government didn't possess a chieftain on a full time basis. On a regular basis, the council would meet to discuss and then decide any decisions that needed to be made. Depending upon their level of importance, these discussions could take days or even weeks before a consensus could finally be reached. Politically, the council couldn't move in any direction unless a solid majority had been obtained. However once a decision had been agreed upon, the heads of the various clans would ensure its compliance and implementation. In the case of war, the council did temporarily select a war leader from its own assembly in order to supervise the campaign. Then once the campaign had been concluded, the war leader would step down from his position and resume his seat on the council. Within this form of government, the decision-making process was actually made into a real procedure. Options were weighed, customs were followed, disagreements and arguments ensued, and decisions were finally ratified before any action was taken on the part of the clans.[33]

Over time, the nomadic council form of government did create and directly impart the idea of utilizing various individuals to oversee certain tasks. This concept of appointing someone from a ruling body to deal with a particular problem would eventually lead to the agrarians instituting the role of the imperial magistrate, as demonstrated by the early Assyrian and Egyptian Empires. The administration of government in the larger agrarian societies would become so immense an undertaking for just one monarch and his or her family to manage that the need for specialized management and administration would increase tenfold. Within their newly formed kingdoms, the average monarch would be forced to seek out the assistance of others who possessed a certain expertise in the fields of politics, economics, religion, engineering, law, or warfare. As a result, the monarchs would eventually broaden these different magistrates' roles into permanent and separate bureaucracies by establishing governmental departments in order to manage their affairs. Even though the agrarians were the first to create governing bureaucracies, they had initially gotten the idea of delegating the monarchs' authority from their nomadic ancestors.[34]

While the nomadic society was as close to a classless society as an economy will permit, it nonetheless would begin to form an upper class. It wasn't an upper class in the true sense of the word, but certain families within the tribe would eventually become more prosperous and more powerful than the other families. Comprised mainly of the tribal leader, the heads of the clans, and the shaman and their relatives, these families not only ruled their societies, but they would also enjoy all of the benefits and privileges entitled to a select group of people. As a result, an elite class was already in place, once we had begun to farm the surrounding fields.[35]

Historically, all human societies in the past and the present have actually been governed and controlled by an elite class. And contrary to popular political rhetoric, it doesn't matter what type of government or economy a society possesses, there still exists a ruling class that oversees, directs, and leads that society. Whether their status has been determined by their wealth, royal heritage, or by their standings within a political party, they form a ruling class that determines the economic, political, and cultural direction of their societies. Hence, the quality of a society's government is not determined by its system or by the type of its legal system, but rather by the quality of people within the society's ruling class, which coincidently directly affects the quality of the people within their government. Whether a society possesses a nomadic, agrarian, or an industrial economy, if that society's ruling class is essentially honest, responsible, benevolent, and farsighted, then that society's government and people will generally follow suit. Throughout human history, the privileged class has represented and reflected the best and the brightest that a culture has had to offer. Unfortunately though, they can also represent the worst. In general, the great civilizations of the past didn't fall due to the greed, indifference, and corruption of the lower classes, but rather from that of the upper classes.[36]

One of the reasons the government, the religious establishments, the educational systems, the courts, and the military are the most conservative and influential institutions in today's societies is because they have a very old nomadic tradition of mutually supporting each other's status quo. If any one of these institutions becomes threatened, as in the case of a civil revolt or a political reform movement, they will inherently protect each other to the bitter end. As discovered by the French, Russia, and Chinese revolutionaries of their time, it wasn't just the government bureaucrats, the police officials, the judges, and the military that they had to overcome. They also had to overcome the religious institutions, the financial establishments, the college administrators, the large land owners, and the different business communities. Historically speaking, a society's institutions aren't separate entities unto themselves that can act independently of each other; any more than a nomadic chief or shaman could ignore or violate the traditions and moral codes of their tribe.[37]

Violence and other deviant behaviors within the nomadic cultures were sanctioned, so long as they were inflicted upon another tribe. The acts of rape, murder, and thievery were quite common between warring parties. Yet, these acts of violence weren't considered actual crimes, but rather as a part of the continuous state of tribal warfare. Thus, the opportunities for a sexually hyper-active male to periodically express these behaviors could explain the nomad's low crime rate within his own tribe. However, this explanation doesn't tell the whole story. Combined with their social customs, religious taboos, and an innately cooperative, sharing culture, it was unthinkable for the average nomad of any gender to resort to violence or inappropriate behaviors. Raised to depend upon everyone around them for their survival, the overwhelming majority of the conflicts within the tribe were caused by either the individual competition for social status or the strained personal relationships brought about by the different clans' competition for tribal control. But overall, their lack of individuality and their adherence to social restrains would make them exceedingly decent citizens.[38]

The tribal laws were very simple, practical, and uncompromising. Based upon our ancestors' improved communication skills, the sources of these laws were a combination of ancient customs, tribal authority, and last but not least, mysticism. In order for them preserve these unwritten laws; the tribal elders would orally transmit them from generation to generation, in much the same manner, as they would educate their children by telling them stories of the past. Crime within the tribe itself was a rare occurrence. The individual's fear of being banished or labeled a nonentity by his or her own people would deter most of the deviant behaviors. And yet, when there was a civil or criminal dispute, it was usually handled by either the tribal council, the head of the tribe, or by the shaman. In any case, judgments were swift, wrongs were rectified, and conflicts were settled.

The nomads discovered quite early in their existence that tribal tranquilly could only be achieved through some form of system or ritual that would dispense justice. Tribal unity was all-important in maintaining their territory and hunting as a coordinated group. Consequently, the need to resolve tribal disputes by granting individuals or clans the right to charge and then summon to court another party for a crime or a civil wrong would become the first rules of law. How the nomadic tribes would go about settling these conflicts or disputes would greatly differ in their procedures or rituals. But, they were the first human societies to create the idea of establishing a set of simple rules (unwritten) to oversee and conduct a semi-legal proceeding.[39]

Governed by ritual and past precedents, it must have taken our ancestors over a millennium to develop their own brand of justice. Each tribe had a different set of rules and obviously a different set of methods. However over time, the more advanced tribes did create an identical set of rules. Whereupon, the civil chief or the tribal council would listen to the accuser state his or her charges against the accused. Then, the accused was given an opportunity to proclaim his or her innocence by presenting the judges with a rebuttal. If there was a conflict of the basic facts, each individual would have an opportunity to present their own evidence to the court. In order for the judge or judges to ascertain the level of accuracy, they possessed the right to cross-examine everyone involved. Then once all of the evidence and witnesses had been presented and cross-examined, the judge or judges would arrive at a verdict for either the accused or the accuser. If the final judgment went against the accused, the punishment could range from forfeiting their tribal privileges and social status to banishing them from the tribe, which would mean almost certain death.[40]

Since the nomads weren't advanced enough to recognize the need for lawyers, juries, and appeals, they nonetheless established the first rules of law. The right to have a semi-legal proceeding, the right to face the accuser, and the right for the accused to defend oneself are all fundamental rights in almost every country in the world today. These basic rights were instituted by many of our later-day nomads for the same reasons that modern societies have instituted them, which is to resolve the population's conflicts by dispensing justice, so as to promote social tranquilly and economic order.

By and large, the nomadic legal system created and helped establish the basic principles and procedures of today's judicial systems. Without a doubt, their proceedings and standards were extremely simple and varied with their superstitious whims, but almost every aspect of a modern trial would have its beginnings from the nomads who held their courts under the bright sunshine.

Between the bordering tribes, the tempo and intensity of their conflicts were the same as their cultural lifestyles, slow paced and methodical. The overwhelming majority of these conflicts occurred, when their hunting parties unexpectedly ran into each other. On occasion, these encounters could very quickly turn into a full-blown skirmish. But normally, the hunters would move off into a different direction, saving their strength and man-power for the purpose of conducting raids against their known enemies. The occasional raid wasn't intended to destroy another people, but rather to drive them away from their territory. Of course, the smaller and weaker tribes had no choice but to give way to the ever-moving tides of war. Almost always outnumbered by their enemies, they eventually found themselves eking out a living in the less fertile territories. So long as they didn't incur the wrath of the more powerful tribes, they were free to continue their way of life.[41]

Not all of the tribes followed the same routine when it came to preparing themselves for a fight. In different parts of the world, the cultural diversity of the tribes revealed itself in their different fetishes, rituals, and spiritual customs. Many of them began to combine a mixture of clays, minerals, and various plant saps in order to paint their bodies with a wide assortment of colorful lines, squares, circles, or other symbols. These symbols were simple and geometric in design. Yet, they could be very intricate, depending upon the painter's expertise. Certain colors like red or black were symbolic of the life and death struggle that these warriors were about to encounter. Much later, many of the nomads would wear a wide variety of elaborate bird feathers, animal bones, horns, teeth, or strips of colorful furs; whereupon signifying their social status, clan identification, or denoting their heroic deeds. As a whole, they were personal symbols that represented several important spiritual aspects of their lives.[42]

The warriors also painted their faces and bodies to appear as ferocious and as frightful as possible. By momentarily paralyzing their enemies with fear and panic, which was a tactic used by their food gathering ancestors, the psychological impact of appearing as death or destruction itself would be of immense value. Frequently overwhelmed and stunned by a warrior's fearsome appearance, an enemy war party could easily be overcome, before they had a chance to regain their senses. In truth, the scarier and crueler a warrior could appear, the easier it was for him to break his opponent's will to resist. And as a rule of thumb, the concept of breaking the enemy's will to resist has always been the cornerstone to military victory. Even today, whoever possesses the most determination and psychological edge, either in combat or in a competitive game, will more than likely come out the victor.[43]

Much like fighting a modern guerilla war, it took a lot of skill and patience to be a successful raider. Usually conducted during the spring and summers months, these raids were very limited in their scope and depth. The casualties were relatively few, since these weren't wars of eradication. Initially fought on the tribes' territorial borders, they actually employed hit and run tactics against each other. But once a war party had successfully ambushed and then killed a significant number of their enemy's hunters, they were able to expand their territory by occupying the abandoned areas. Over time, it became very common for the victors to collect war trophies from their dead victims and wear them as ornaments. Within their world-view, the taking of trophies such as ears, eyes, genitals, fingers, toes, or even hair from their enemy's bodies would enhance their personal and spiritual power.[44]

When it came to fighting another hominid species like the Neanderthals, our ancestors probably did engage in wars of eradication. Once their enemy's outer camps had been destroyed and abandoned by their persistent raiding, our ancestors were in position to launch a number of incursion campaigns that went deeper and deeper into the enemy's territory. The strategic purpose behind these incursions was very different than conducting a simple raid. Instead of harassing and ambushing the enemy's hunters on the outer fringes of their territory with a small number of warriors, the incursion was organize and then carried out by numerous war parties in order to literally overrun and destroy their enemy's main campsites. Similar to an anaconda squeezing the life out of its prey, the constant raiding followed by the incursion campaign would slowly drain the life's blood out of their enemies by systematically eliminating their man-power and food resources. By coordinating and implementing the outer raids and then the deep incursions, the our ancestors were able to conduct fairly effective campaigns of extermination against their most hated and fearful enemies.[45]

To this day, it isn't entirely known how and why the H. s. neanderthensis disappeared. Although, there are several European sagas and legends of them existing up to the Dark and Early Middle Ages, the archaeological evidence indicts that they suddenly disappeared approximately 30,000 to 35,000 years ago. Much like the disappearance of the dinosaurs, there are many theories as to why they suddenly vanished. Some scientists believe they disappeared through our genetic absorption as if we were all one big happy family. While a few others have theorized that a massive volcano erupted around 40,000 years ago in the vicinity of Naples, Italy, thus causing a volcanic winter that led to their starvation, but ironically not that of our own species. Then, there are scientists who believe the Neanderthals were already becoming extinct, due to their inability to adapt to the climatic changes occurring across Eurasia during that same period. Unfortunately, this belief is based upon the premise that the Neanderthals weren't a very adaptable species, which is contrary to the archaeological evidence.[46]

In all probability, there were several interrelated causes behind the Neanderthal's demise. And yet, our ancestors undoubtedly played an important role behind it. As the competition for food intensified with the disappearance of the vast herds during this last glaciation (Wurm-Weichselian) period, it would have created an irreversible and desperate conflict between the two species. As a result, our ancestors eventually emerged as the victors in a winner take all conflict that could have lasted well over 10,000 years. Along with our ancestors' superior ability to communicate with each other and the immense advantage of having organizing themselves into tribes, this victory could have also been easily accomplished with their invention of the bow and arrow, around 60,000 years ago.[47]

There can be little doubt that our forefathers and foremothers wouldn't have found any common ground or a cultural attachment to the Neanderthals. Ironically, there were many physical and cultural similarities between us, but there were also an abundance of major differences. As nomadic competitors, our ancestors would have looked upon them as a threat to very their existence. By employing the deep incursions as part of their military campaigns, they could have easily conducted a successful war of eradication against them. However, this type of warfare wouldn't have produced any huge battles or prolonged sieges. Instead, it would have been methodically carried out to the point where the Neanderthals eventually became extinct. Considering the circumstances, this conflict was not only a struggle over territory, but it was possibly an extreme form of genocide, where the viciousness and blind brutality towards each other would have been unlimited.[48]

Although, the nomads helped develop many of our present military tactics, their conflicts weren't conventional wars in the modern sense of the word. Unlike the later-day agrarian Egyptian, Assyrian, Chinese, Greek, or Roman civilizations, they didn't form large well-equipped armies nor did their commanders attempt to force a decision by engaging the enemy in a drawn-out battle. However, it would be a huge mistake to view nomadic warfare as a primitive and unsophisticated way of fighting. It took a lot of skill, organization, and imagination by the nomads to be successful at it. As skilled horsemen, the later-day nomadic Mongols (1206-1368) would eventually establish the largest land empire in human history. It was larger than the Greek and Roman Empires had ever dreamed of conquering, covering close to 13 million square miles. And much like these earlier Mediterranean empires, the nomads would use a mixture of terror, bribery, diplomacy, and naked force to obtain their goals.[49]

The nomadic economy didn't create any congested cities, long winding roads, or even busy factories. The mobility of the tribes and the necessity to travel light over long distances greatly limited their need or their desire to produce a large quality of surpluses. Their economic motivation wasn't based upon profit, but rather upon their survival and the communal good. Of course, the nomadic way of life has nearly become a lost relic of the past. But its impact upon our physical and cultural evolution has been immeasurable.

It must be remembered that we embraced the nomadic economy for over 99% of our existence and that its profound influences can be felt even unto today. In a very real sense, it instigated our biological and physiological development from a clumsy semi-erect creature to our present physical form. Along with enhancing our ability to orally communicate with each other, it also helped further develop our hands and minds, whereby enhancing our evolutionary feedback loops.

As a consequence, it was an economy that ultimately induced our nomadic families to develop the economic skills to produce simple weapons, tools, clothing, jewelry, and other items, along with the opportunities to trade them. But more importantly, it created the basic foundations of our present day institutions by establishing our first governments (clan and tribal leaders) and our first religions (animisms and mysticisms). Moreover, it produced our first religious leaders and doctors (shamans and healers), teachers (parents), and our first judges (civil chiefs) and legal systems. It also helped establish the whole cultural concept of family unity by creating pair-bonding and then the institution of marriage. And finally, it initiated our first business enterprises (traders) and that of our first military forces (war parties), which protect our way of life. While existing in a world where life was cheap, justice was simple and brutal, and their survival was ever so uncertain, our nomadic ancestors unknowingly initiated the genesis of our future civilizations.

For almost 2 million years, our Paleolithic ancestors struggled and even thrived within a violent and exceedingly harsh world. Born under the sun and stars, they survived every known natural disaster by their sheer fortitude, determination, and resourcefulness. Strengthened by the bonds of their families, they took no orders except by choice. As untamed creatures endeavoring to find more bountiful surroundings, they walked the land and crossed the rivers and mountains as free spirits. As they worshipped the mysterious powers around them and looked up into the night sky in wonder, they build their shelters, made their weapons and tools, and buried their dead. While raising their children as loving and caring parents, they gleefully brutalized their enemies.

They were valiant in their pursuits, incredibly adaptable, and utterly ruthless in obtaining their goals. Amid an unsympathetic and unforgiving predatory world, they continued to sacrifice and survive, due to the roaming economy they had created and the cultural paths that they had chosen to follow. Immensely proud of their peoples' emerging heritages, these offspring of the "Titans of the Forests" stood at the apex of the animal kingdom. They should be remembered, revered, and even honored as long as modern men and women have the foresight to look back into our prehistoric past and marvel at their success.

Foot Notes

Chapter One

1. Dougal Dixon, Ian Jenkins, Richard T. Moody, and Andrew Yu. Zhuravlev, Atlas of Life on Earth, (New York: Barnes & Noble Books, 2001), 214-215.
2. Ibid., 216-217.
3. Donald R. Prothero, After the Dinosaurs: The Age of Mammals, (Bloomington, IN: Indiana University Press, 2006), 35.
4. Dixon, Jenkins, Moody, and Zhuravlev, 222-223.
5. Ibid., 224.
6. Charles Frankel, The End of the Dinosaurs: Chicxulub Crater and Mass Extinctions, (Cambridge, UK: Cambridge University Press, 1999), 6.
7. Ibid., 102-112.
8. Walter Alvarez, T-Rex and the Crater of Doom, (Princeton, NJ: Princeton University Press, 1997), 12.
9. Ibid., 13-14.
10. Frankel, 135-140.
11. Ibid., 37-47.
12. Dixon, Jenkins, Moody, and Zhuravlev, 53-58.
13. Ibid., 176-177.
14. Prothero, 53-58.
15. Dixon, Jenkins, Moody, and Zhuravlev, 270-271.
16. Ibid., 280-281.
17. Ibid., 251-253.

18. Ibid., 281-283.

19. Desmond Morris, The Naked Ape, (New York: Random House, 1967), 20-21.

20. J.R. Minkel, Human- Chimp: Gene Gap Widens from Talley of Duplicate Genes, (London, UK: Scientific American Magazine, 2006).
    http://www.scientificamerican.com/article.cfm?id=human-chimp-gene-gap-wide

21. Chris Stringer and Peter Andrews, The Complete World of Human Evolution, (New York: Thames & Hudson Inc., 2012), 12-13.

22. Ibid., 114-116.
    A) Colin Tudge, The Time Before History: 5 Million Years of Human Impact. (New York: Scribner, 1996), 184-185.

23. Noel Boaz, Eco Homo: How the Human Being Emerged from the   Cataclysmic History of Earth, (New York: Basic Books, 1997), 89-98.

24. Stringer and Andrews, 13.

25. G.J. Sawyer and Viktor Deak, The Last Human, (New Haven, CT: Yale University Press, 2007), 20-21.

26. Boaz, 114.

27. Craig Stanford, The Hunting Apes: Meat Eating and the Origins of Human Behavior, (Princeton, NJ: Princeton University Press. 1999), 15-16.

28. Ibid., 93-94.

29. Stringer and Andrews, 53-57.

30. Dixon, Jenkins, Moody, and Zhuravlev, 288-289.

Chapter Two

Frans De Waal, Our Inner Ape, (New York: Riverhead Books, 2005), 1-7.

2. Robert Jenkins, Director, Chimpanzee, (Salina, KS: Rolling Hills Wild Life Adventure Zoo, 2013).

   http://www.rollinghillswildlife.com/animals/c/chimpanzee/

3. Ibid., 1.

4. Jane Goodall, The Chimpanzees of Gombe: Patterns of Behavior, (Cambridge MA: Belknap Press of Harvard University, 1986), 28-34.

5. Ibid., 36-37, 559-560.

6. Ibid., 38-42.

7. Ibid., 376-386.

8. Goodall, In the Shadow of Man, (New York: Houghton Mifflin Co. 1970), 273-276.

9. Goodall, Chimpanzees of Gombe: Patterns of Behavior, 283.

10. Ibid., 284-285.

11. Tattersall, 13-19.

12. Goodall, Chimpanzees of Gombe: Patterns of Behavior, 338.

13. Ibid., 555-557.

14. Ibid., 228-230.

15. Ibid., 241.

16. Ibid., 232-236.

17. Craig Stanford, Chimpanzee Hunting Behavior and Human Evolution, (Triangle Park, NC: American Scientist Magazine, May-June 1995), 1-3.

http://www.americanscientist.org/issues/pub/chimpanzee-hunting-behavior-and-human-evolution/

18. Ibid., 2-4.

19. David Attenborough, Chimpanzees Team Up to Attack Monkeys in the Wild,   (United Kingdom, UK: BBC Planet Earth Wildlife, April 2008).
http://www.youtube.com/watch?v=A1WBs74W4ik

20. Goodall, Chimpanzees of Gombe: Patterns of Behavior, 290-299.

21. Ibid., 300, 372-376.

22. Goodall, In the Shadow of Man, 277-280.

23. Goodall, Chimpanzees of Gombe: Patterns of Behavior, 536-537

24. Goodall, Shadows of Man, 29-30, 209-210.

25. Goodall, Chimpanzees of Gombe: Patterns of Behavior, 544-549.

26. Ibid., 549-551.

27. Ibid., 413-415, 424-429.

28. Ibid., 415-418.

29. Ibid., 437-439.

30. Frans De Waal and Frans Lanting, Bonobo: The Forgotten Ape, (Los Angeles, CA: University of California Press, 1998), 101-105.

31. Goodall, Chimpanzees of Gombe: Patterns of Behavior, 447-448.

32. Ibid., 86-87, 443, 451, 466-470.

33. De Waal, Our Inner Ape, 114-115.

34. Goodall, Chimpanzees of Gombe: Patterns of Behavior 84, 450-453.
A) Goodall, In the Shadow of Man, 186-187.

35. Goodall, Chimpanzees of Gombe: Patterns of Behavior, 530-534.

36. Ibid., 84-86, 444.

37. Ibid., 101-104.

38. Ibid., 147-148.

39. Ibid., 379.

40. Ibid., 263-266, 560-564.

41. Goodall, In the Shadows of Man, 150-151.

42. Ibid., 155-158.

43. Goodall, Chimpanzees of Gombe: Patterns of Behavior, 369-373.

44. Ibid., 489-500.
   A) Craig Stanford, The Chimpanzee Hunting Behavior and
   Human Evolution,34.
   http://www.americanscientist.org/issues/pub/chimpanzee-
   hunting-behavior-and-human-evolution/

45. Goodall, Chimpanzees of Gombe, 513-519.

46. Ibid., 530-534.

Chapter Three

1. Ian Tattersall, Masters of the Planet: The Search for Human Origins,
   (New York: Palgrave Macmillan, 2012), 3.

2. Ibid., 6.

3. Sawyer and Deak, 19-20.

4. Tattersall, 1-2.

5. Stringer and Andrews, 117-134.

6. Boaz, 114-117.

7. Alice Roberts, Evolution: The Human Story, (London, UK: Dorling
   Kindersley
   Limited, 2011), 76-85.
   A) Sawyer and Deak, 65-74.

8. Richard Wrangham and Dale Peterson, Demonic Males: Apes and the Origins of Human Violence, (New York: Houghton Mifflin Co. 1996), 216-217.

9. Tattersall, 38-39.
   A) Zeresenay Alemseged and Shannon McPherron, Scientists Discover Oldest Evidence of Human Stone Tool Use and Meat-eating, (Leipzig, Germany: 2010).
   http://www.eurekalert.org/pub_releases/2010-08/m-sdo081210.php

10. Tattersall, 59-61.

11. Ibid., 26-29.

12. Boaz, 123-125.

13. Ibid., 114.
    A) Sawyer and Deak, 79-84.

14. Sawyer and Deak, 87-96.

15. Roberts, Evolution: The Human Story, 88-92.
    A) Evolution, Nova, WGBH Foundation, 2001.
    http://www.pbs.org/wgbh/evolution/humans/humankind/h.html

16. Boaz, 143-144.

17. Stanford, The Hunting Apes: Meat Eating and the Origins of Human Behavior, 124-125.

18. Tattersall, 54-56.

19. Stanford, The Hunting Apes: Meat Eating and the Origins of Human Behavior, 126-128.

20. Ibid., 111-117.

21. Boaz, 161-163.

22. Tattersall, 51.

23. Stanford, The Hunting Apes: Meat Eating and the Origins of Human Behavior, 202-203.

24. Wrangham and Peterson, 71-77.

25. Goodall, Chimpanzees of Gombe: Patterns of Behavior, 513-519.

26. Dixon, Jenkins, Moody, and Zhuravlev, 294-304.

27. Tattersall, 84-89.

28. Sigfried De Laet, J. Editor, History of Humanity, Prehistory and the Beginnings of Civilization, Volume 1, (New York: Chapman and Hall Inc. 1994). 31-32.
A) Sawyer and Deak, 124.
B) Evolution, Nova, WGBH Foundation, 2001.
http://www.pbs.org/wgbh/evolution/humans/humankind/j.html
C) Suzanne Kemmer, The Origin and Evolution of Human Language, 2012
http://www.ruf.rice.edu/~kemmer/Evol/habiliserectus.html

29. Nicholas Wade. Before the Dawn: Recovering the Lost History of Our Ancestors. (New York: Penguin Books, 2006), 37-40.
A) Tudge, 246-250.
B) Fossil Hominids, Talk Origins Archives, 2011.
http://www.talkorigins.org/faqs/homs/species.html#habilis

30. Wade, 43-47.
A) Tudge, 251-252.

31. Tattersall, 214-217.
A) Boaz, 165-166.

32. Sawyer and Deak, 127-128.
A) Stanford, The Hunting Apes: Meat Eating and the Origins of Human Behavior, 110-112.

33. Roberts, Evolution: The Human Story, 102-103.

34. The Oldowan Stone Tool Industry, (Berkeley, CA: University of California, Berkeley, 2013).
http://www.lithiccastinglab.com/gallery-pages/oldowanstonetools.htm

35. Boaz, 162-166.

36. Stringer and Andrews, 68-71.

37. Tudge, 204-209.

Chapter Four

1. Dixon, Jenkins, Moody, and Zhuravlev, 300-301.
   A) Evolution, Nova, WGBH Foundation, 2001.
   http://www.pbs.org/wgbh/nova/earth/cause-ice-age.html

2. Tudge, 38-39.

3. Doug Macdougall, Frozen Earth: The Once and Future Story of
   the Ices Ages. (Berkeley, CA: University of California Press,
   1994), 9-13.
   A) Stephen Nelson, Glaciers and Glaciations, (New Orleans, LA:
   Tulane University, 2003).
   http://www.tulane.edu/~sanelson/geol111/glaciers.htm

4. Dixon, Jenkins, Moody, and Zhuravlev, 302-304.

5. Macdougall, 89-90.

6. Tatterall, 146-147.

7. Boaz, 171.
   A) Tudge, 213.
   B) Donald Johnson, Origins of Modern Humans: Multiregional
   or Out of Africa. (American Institute of Biological Sciences,
   2001).
   http://www.actionbioscience.org/evolution/johanson.html
   C) Becoming Human Part II, PBS Video, 2009.
   http://video.pbs.org/video/1319997127/

8. Boaz, 176-179.
   A) Dennis O'Neil, Early Human Evolution. (San Marcos, CA:
   Behavioral Science Department, Palomar College, 2013).
   http://anthro.palomar.edu/homo/homo_2.htm

9. Tudge, 225.
   A) O'Neil, Early Human Evolution, 2013.
   http://anthro.palomar.edu/homo2/mod_homo_1.htm

10. Roberts, Evolution: The Human Story, 124-125.

11. Ibid., 126-127.

12. Tudge, 210-211.

13. Ibid., 212-213.

14. J.M. Roberts and Odd Arne Westad, The History of the World,
    6th Edition, (New York: Oxford University Press, 2013), 15-17.
    A) Chris Stringer, Lone Survivors: How We Came To Be the
    Only Humans on Earth, (New York: Time Books, 2012), 89-90.

15. Tudge, 205-7.

16. Ibid., 245.

17. Boaz, 178.

18. Richard Klein and Edgar Blake, The Dawn of Human Culture,
    (New York: John Wiley & Sons, 2002), 157-161.
    A) Sawyer and Deak, 139-140.
    B) http://www.citizendia.org/Acheulean

19. Tattersall, 139-140.
    A) Jeremy Norman, From Cave Paintings to the Internet,
    History of Information, 2013.
    http://www.historyofinformation.com/expanded.php

20. Stringer, Lone Survivors: How We Came To Be the Only
    Humans on Earth, 144-145.
    A) Tattersall., 111-113.

21. Boaz, 179-181.

22. Jonathan Shaw, Evolution by Fire: Primitive Protection Racket,
    (Cambridge, Massachusetts: Harvard Magazine, 2009).

23. Tudge, 259-263.

24. O'Neil, Early Human Evolution, 2013.
    http://anthro.palomar.edu/homo/homo_2.htm

25. Stanford, The Hunting Apes: Meat Eating and the Origins of
    Human Behavior, 203-04.
    A) The Origins of Government, The American Republic,
    Chapter 3, 2008.
    http://terrenceberres.com/broame03.html

26. Jared Diamond, The Third Chimpanzee: The Evolution and
    Future of the Human Animal, (New York: Harper Publishers,
    1992), 142.
    A) Tudge, 246-250.

27. Kent V. Flannery, Prehistoric Social Evolution, 2013.
    http://depthome.brooklyn.cuny.edu/anthro/faculty/mitrovic/
    Flannery.pdf p 5.

28. Goodall, Chimpanzees of Gombe: Patterns of Behavior, 147-148.

29. Ibid., 290-299.

30. Family Values, National Institute of Mathematics and Biological
    Sciences, USA, 2012.
    http://www.nimbios.org/press/FS_pair-bonding

31. De Waal, 108.

32. Allen Johnson, and Timothy Earl, The Evolution of Human
    Societies: The Evolution of Human Societies from Foraging
    Group to Agrarian State, (Stanford, CA: Stanford University
    Press, 2000), 46-49.
    A) Anthology of Ideas, Culture Based on Instinct: Creation of
    the Human Family, 2006.
    http://www.historyofinformation.com/expanded.php

33. Time, Health and Family, 2012.
    http://healthland.time.com/2012/05/29/the-ancient-sexual-
    revolution-that-may-have-spurred-human-monogamy/

34. Boaz, 196-197.

35. Tudge, 256-257.

36. Humans Hunted for Meat 2 Million Years Ago, The
    Guardian/Observer, 2012.
    http://www.theguardian.com/science/2012/sep/23/human-
    hunting-evolution-2million-years

37. How to Track Animals, WikiHow, 2012.
    http://www.wikihow.com/Track-Animals

38. Stanford, The Hunting Apes: Meat Eating and the Origins of
    Human Behavior, 149.

39. Sawyer and Deak, 141, 158-159.

40. Stringer, Lone Survivors: How We Came To Be the Only
    Humans on Earth, 88-91.

41. E.O. James, Prehistoric Religion, (New York: Barnes & Noble,
    Inc. 1957), 17-18.
    A) Klein and Blake, 138-140.

Chapter Five

1. Roberts, Evolution: The Human Story, 128-131.
   A) Tattersall, 152-154.

2. Ibid., 184.
   A) The Smithsonian National Museum of Natural History,
   (Washington, D.C.: 2013).
   http://humanorigins.si.edu/evidence/human-
   fossils/species/homo-heidelbergensis
   B) The Natural History Museum, (London, UK: 2011).
   http://www.nhm.ac.uk/nature-online/life/human-
   origins/early-human family/homo-heidelbergensis/index.html

3. Roberts, Evolution: The Human Story, 136-137.
   A) O'Neil, Early Human Evolution, 2013.
   http://anthro.palomar.edu/homo2/mod_homo_1.htm

B) Hominid Species, The Talk Origins Archive, 2010.
http://www.talkorigins.org/faqs/homs/species.html#archaics

4. Klein and Blake, 156-157.

5. Kate O' Looney, Fire as a Symbol of Religion, (Spokane, WA: Gonzaga University 2012).
http://gonzagakate.tripod.com/id12.html

6. T. R. Fehrenbach, Comanches: The History of a People, (New York: Anchor Books 2003), 46-47.

7. Incest, Reference.com, 2013.
http://www.reference.com/browse/incest

8. Fehrenbach, 38.

9. Ibid., 36-37.

10. The Role of the Father, Scribd.com, Fifth Edition, 2011.
http://www.scribd.com/doc/28495112/The-Role-of-the-Father-in-Child-Development

11. Strong Fathers as Strong Teachers, Strongfathers.com, 2013.
http://strongfathers.com/strong-fathers-as-strong-teachers-3/

12. Stringer, Lone Survivors: How We Came To Be the Only Humans on Earth, 158-159.

13. The Concept of Yin & Yang in Chinese Culture, eHow.com, 2011.
http://www.ehow.com/facts_6744680_concept-yin-yang-chinese-culture.html

14. Ibid., 1.

15. Alice H. Eagly and Wendy Wood, The Origins of Sex Differences in Human Behavior, (College Station, TX: Texas A&M University, 2013).
http://www.sscnet.ucla.edu/anthro/faculty/fiske/facets/eagly&wood.htm

16. Ibid., 1.

17. William Masters, Virginia Johnson, and Robert C. Kolodny, Human Sexuality, 5th Edition, (New York: Harper Collins College Publishers, 1995), 276–277.

18. Ibid., 87-89, 277-278.

19. Ibid., 87, 279.

20. Sarah Shiver Hughes and Bradley Hughes, Women in Ancient Civilizations, (Philadelphia, PA: Temple University Press, 2001), 118-119.

21. What is a Matriarchy, Origin of Sexism, 2012. http://originofsexism.blogspot.com/2012/03/what-is-matriarchy.html

22. Klein and Edgar, 267.

Chapter Six

1. Macdougall, 187-189.
    A) O'Neil, Early Human Evolution, 2013.
    http://anthro.palomar.edu/homo/homo_3.htm

2. Tatterall, 146-148.

3. Roberts, Evolution: The Human Story, 164.
    A) O'Neil, Early Human Evolution, 2013.
    http://anthro.palomar.edu/homo/homo_3.htm

4. Milford Wolpoff, John Hawks, and Rachel Caspari, Multiregional, Not Multiple Origins, (Ann Arbor, MI: Department of Anthropology, University of Michigan, 2000).
    http://www-personal.umich.edu/~wolpoff/Papers/Multiregional.PDF
    B) Donald Johnson, Origins of Modern Humans: Multiregional or Out of Africa. (American Institute of Biological Sciences, 2001).
    http://www.actionbioscience.org/evolution/johanson.html

5. Tudge, 225-232.
   A). Paul Rincon, Humans Left Africa Much Earlier, BBC,
   Science and the Environment, 2011.
   http://www.bbc.co.uk/news/science-environment-12300228
   B) Out of Africa Theory, Metapedia, 2013.
   http://en.metapedia.org/wiki/Out_of_Africa_theory
   C) Out of Africa? Data Fails to Support Language Origin in
   Africa, Science Daily, 2013.
   http://www.sciencedaily.com/releases/2012/02/120215143001
   .htm

6. Roberts, Evolution: The Human Story, 165-166.

7. Lawrence Keeley, War Before Civilization: The Myth of the
   Peaceful Savages. (Oxford, UK: Oxford University Press, 1996),
   51-53.
   A) Amanda Briney, The last Glaciation, About.com. Geography
   and Education, 2013.
   http://geography.about.com/od/climate/a/glaciation.htm

8. Sigfried De Laet, Editor, History of Humanity, Prehistory and the
   Beginnings of Civilization, Volume 1, (New York: Chapman and
   Hall Inc. 1994), 120-121.
   A). Roberts, Evolution: The Human Story, 166.

9. Tatterall, 98-99.

10. Shere Hite, Opedipus Revisited, (London, UK: Arcadia Books,
    2005), 8-10, 30-31.

11. Masters, Johnson, and Kolodny, 87, 210-211.

12. Ibid., 54.
    A) Goodall, In the Shadows of Man, 79.

13. Masters, Johnson, and Kolodny, 114-117.

14. Ibid., 118-124.

15. Stef Daniels, A Mother's Instinct, The Professor's House. 2012.
    http://www.professorshouse.com/Family/Motherhood/Article
    s/A-Mothers-Instinct/

16. Homosexuality in the Ancient World, Knowledge Guild, 2013. http://knowledgeguild.wordpress.com/2013/07/01/homosexuality-in-the-ancient-world/

17. Masters, Johnson, and Kolodny, 217, 379-384.

18. Sexual bondage: A Review and Unobtrusive Investigation, U.S. National Library of Science 1995. http://www.ncbi.nlm.nih.gov/pubmed/8572912

19. Fehrenbach, 31.

20. Ibid., 32.
    A) Boaz, 228-229.

21. Roger Walsh, The World of Shamanism, (Woodbury, MN: Llewellyn Publications, 2007), 17-19, 126-129.

22. Ibid., 133-136.
    A) Fehrenbach, 47-51.

23. Fehrenbach, 51-56.

24. Superstitions and Their Origins, Manali Oak, 2011. http://www.buzzle.com/articles/superstitions-and-their-origins.html

25. Piers Vitebsky, Shamanism, (Norman, OK: University of Oklahoma Press, 2001), 8-14.
    A) Roberts, Evolution: The Human Story, 167.

26. Wesley A. Niewoehner, Behavioral Inferences from the Skhul/Qafzeh Early Modern Human Hand Remains, Washington D.C.: National Academy of the Sciences, 2000. http://www.pnas.org/content/98/6/2979.full

27. Vitebsky, 10-11, 50-51.

28. Welsh, 49-54.

29. Michael Hamer, Shamanism, the Role of the Shaman, Religion and Spiritual Beliefs Resource, 2013. http://www.important.ca/shamanism_role_of_a_shaman.html

30. Fehrenbach, 35-37, 55.

31. Albert Lyons, Primitive Medicine, Health Guidance, 2013.
    http://www.healthguidance.org/entry/6306/1/Primitive-
    Medicine.html

32. Vitebsky, 98-101.

33. Keeley, 95-97.

34. Welsh, 208-211.
    A) Vitebsky, 147-148.

35. Vitebsky, 88-89, 207-208.
    A) Rick Martin, Dyslexic Shaman, 2013.
    http://dyslexicshaman.com/shaman.html

36. Roberts and Westad, The History of the World, 54-58.

37. Fehranbach, 23-24, 41-42.

38. War and Terrorism in the Animal Kingdom, Education and
    Science, 2011.
    http://athena09.hubpages.com/hub/War-and-Terrorism-in-
    the-Animal-Kingdom

39. Fehrenbach, 63-64.
    A) Keeley, 32-33.

40. Fehrenbach, 68-69.
    A) Keeley, 108-116.

41. Fehrenbach, 62-63.
    A) Keeley, 65-66.

42. Keeley, 46-47.

43. Ibid., 46-47.

44. Stringer, Lone Survivors: How We Came To Be the Only
    Humans on Earth, 158-160.

Chapter Seven

1. Stringer and Andrews, 212-15.
   A) Stringer, Lone Survivors: How We Came To Be the Only Humans on Earth, 121-126.
   B) Boaz, 230-235.

2. Jared Diamond, Guns, Germs, and Steel: The Fate of Human Societies, (New York: W.W. Norton, 1997), 39.
   A) Tudge, 205-207, 245.
   B) The Great Leap Forward, Behavior Modernity, 2013.
   http://en.wikipedia.org/wiki/Behavioral_modernity#Great_lea p_forward

3. Stringer and Andrews, 20-21.
   A) Roberts, History of the World, 27.

4. Stringer and Andrews, 22-23.
   A) M.H. Wolfoff, Modern Human Origins, Science Magazine, 1988.
   http://www.sciencemag.org/content/241/4867/772

5. C) How many major races are there in the world? World mysteries, 2011.
   http://blog.world-mysteries.com/science/how-many-major-races-are-there-in-the-world/

6. Stringer, Lone Survivors: How We Came To Be the Only Humans on Earth, 186-188.
   A) Diamond, The Third Chimpanzee: The Evolution and Future of the Human Animal, 110-114.
   B) R.C. Lewontin, Confusions about Human Races, 2006.
   http://raceandgenomics.ssrc.org/Lewontin/
   C) Michael White, What Our Genes Tell Us About Race, 2008.
   http://www.science20.com/adaptive_complexity/what_our_ge nes_tell_us_about_race

7. Stringer and Andrews, 188-190.

8. Boaz, 228-229.
   A) Diamond, The Third Chimpanzee: The Evolution and Future
   of the Human Animal, 236.

9. Raymond S. Nickerson, Confirmation Bias: A Ubiquitous
   Phenomenon in Many Guises, Tufts University, 1998.
   http://psy2.ucsd.edu/~mckenzie/nickersonConfirmationBias.
   pdf

10. Fehrenbach, 137.
    A) David Wishart, Great Plains Indians, (Lincoln, NB: University
    of Nebraska Press, 2007), 204-205.

11. Tuareg People, Bonded Castes and Slaves, 2013.
    http://en.wikipedia.org/wiki/Tuareg_people

12. Slavery in the Ancient World, Fact Monster Encyclopedia, 2012.
    http://www.factmonster.com/encyclopedia/business/slavery-
    history.html

13. History of Slavery, Reference.com, 2008.
    http://www.reference.com/browse/slavery

14. Tudge, 215.
    A) Stringer, Lone Survivors: How We Came To Be the Only
    Humans on Earth, 54-58, 196-199.
    B) Klein and Blake, 172-178.
    C) Richard Scroggins, The Truth About Cro-Magnon, 2013.
    http://voices.yahoo.com/the-truth-cro-magnon-
    12360825.html

15. Fehrenbach, 249.

16. Wishart, 211.
    A) Gregory S. Chora, Ancient Trade and Civilization, 2009.
    http://www.aurlaea.com/article-177-
    ancient_trade_and_civilization.html

17. Diamond, The Third Chimpanzee: The Evolution and Future of
    the Human Animal, 48-49.
    A) History, Trade, and Art, Prehistoric Trade, 2010.

http://historytradeart.blogspot.com/2010/05/prehistoric-trade.html

18. Stringer, Lone Survivors: How We Came To Be the Only Humans on Earth, 157-158.

19. Kisholoy Mukherjee, Evolution of Family and Marriage, 2013. http://www.scribd.com/doc/178337843/Evolution-of-Family-and-Marriage

20. Ancient History/Human Evolution/Neolithic Age, Wikibooks, 2013. http://en.wikibooks.org/wiki/Ancient_History/Human_Evolution/Neolithic_Age

21. A History of Human Culture, Evolution, Psychology, and Culture, 2012. http://www.onelife.com/psy/culhist.html A) Ancient History/Human Evolution/Neolithic Age, Wikibooks, 2013 http://en.wikibooks.org/wiki/Ancient_History/Human_Evolution/Neolithic_Age

22. Wishart, 153.

23. Ibid., 154.

24. Johnson and Earle, 34-35.

25. Roberts and Westad, The History of the World, 60-61.

26. Johnson and Earle, 32-33.

27. Wishart, 48. A) Fehrenbach, 43-46.

28. Michael Hamer, Shamanism, the Role of the Shaman, Religion and Spiritual Beliefs Resource, 2013. http://www.important.ca/shamanism_role_of_a_shaman.html

29. Welsh, 49-54.

30. Wishart, 153-154.

31. Ibid., 182.

32. Roberts, The History of the World, 60-61, 63-66, 70-71.

33. Wishart, 142, 185.

34. Roberts, The History of the World, 73, 108-110.

35. Johnson and Earle, 34-35.

36. Ibid., 26-29.

37. Roberts, The History of the World, 732-747, 895-896, 916-930.

38. Johnson and Earle, 61, 75.

39. Wishart, 113-114.

40. Ibid., 114-115.

41. Fehrenbach, 62.

42. Ibid., 72.

43. War Paint, Native American Encyclopedia, 2013.
    http://nativeamericanencyclopedia.com/war-paint/

44. Keeley, 99-103, 127-129.

45. Ibid., 66-69.

46. Tudge, 215.
    A) Stringer, Lone Survivors: How We Came To Be the Only
    Humans on Earth, 54-58.

47. Diamond, The Third Chimpanzee: The Evolution and Future of
    the Human Animal, 51-54.
    A) Keeley, 103-106,
    B) Michael Balter, Humans Blamed for Neanderthals
    Extinction, (New York: Science Now Magazine, 2012).
    http://www.wired.com/wiredscience/2012/07/neanderthal-
    extinction-human-caused/

48. Klein and Blake, 138-140.
    A) Annalee Newitz, What Modern Humans Can Learn From the

Neanderthals' Extinction, (New York: Popular Science
Magazine, 2013).
http://www.popsci.com/science/article/2013-05/how-avoid-
meeting-neanderthals-fate
A) Stringer, Lone Survivors: How We Came To Be the Only
Humans on Earth, 54-58, 196-199.

49. Stringer, Lone Survivors: How We Came To Be the Only
Humans on Earth, 167-160.
A) Roberts, The History of the World, 37, 389-397.

Bibliography

1. Alemseged, Zeresenay and Shannon McPherron. Scientists Discover Oldest Evidence of Human Stone Tool Use and Meat-eating. Leipzig, Germany: Dikika Research Project, 2010.

2. Alvarez, Walter. T-Rex and the Crater of Doom. Princeton, NJ: Princeton University Press, 1997.

3. Attenborough, David. Chimpanzees Team up to Attack a Monkey in the Wild. London, UK: BBC Planet Earth Wildlife, April 2008.

4. Balter, Michael. Humans Blamed for Neanderthals Extinction. Washington D.C.: Science Now Magazine, 2012.

5. Boaz, Noel. Eco Homo: How the Human Being Emerged from the Cataclysmic History of Earth. New York: Basic Books, 1997.

6. De Waal, Frans. Our Inner Ape. New York: Riverhead Books, 2005.

7. De Waal, Frans and Frans Lanting. Bonobo: The Forgotten Ape. Los Angeles, CA: University of California Press, 1997.

8. De Laet, Sigfried, J. History of Humanity, Prehistory and the Beginnings of Civilization. Volume 1, New York: Chapman and Hall Inc. 1994.

9. Diamond, Jared. The Third Chimpanzee: The Evolution and Future of the Human Animal. New York: Harper Publishers, 1992.

10. Diamond, Jared. Guns, Germs, and Steel: The Fate of Human Societies. New York: W. W. Norton, 1997.

11. Dixon, Dougal, Ian Jenkins, Richard T. Moody, and Andrew Yu. Zhuravlev. Atlas of Life on Earth. New York: Barnes & Noble Books, 2001.

12. Eagly, Alice H. and Wendy Wood. The Origins of Sex Differences in Human Behavior. College Station, TX: Texas A&M University, 2013.

13. Fehrenbach, T. R. Comanches: The History of a People. New York: Anchor Books, 2003.

14. Frankel, Charles. The End of the Dinosaurs: Chicxulub Crater and Mass Extinctions. Cambridge, UK: Cambridge University Press, 1999.

15. Goodall, Jane. In the Shadow of Man. New York: Houghton Mifflin Co. 1972.

16. Goodall, Jane. The Chimpanzees of Gombe: Patterns of Behavior. Cambridge, MA: Belknap Press of Harvard University, 1986.

17. Graeber, David. Debt: The First 5,000 Years. Brooklyn, New York: Melville House Publishing, 2011.

18. Hamer, Michael. Shamanism: the Role of the Shaman. New York: Religion and Spiritual Beliefs Resource, 2013.

19. Hite, Shere. Opedipus Revisited. London, UK: Arcadia Books, 2005.

20. Hughes, Sarah Shiver and Bradley Hughes. Women in Ancient Civilizations. Philadelphia, PA: Temple University Press, 2001.

21. James, E.O. Prehistoric Religion. New York: Barnes & Noble, Inc. 1957.

22. Jenkins, Robert. Rolling Hills Wild Life Adventure Zoo. Salina, KS: 2013.

23. Johnson, Allen and Timothy Earl. The Evolution of Human Societies from Foraging Group to Agrarian State. Stanford, CA: Stanford University Press, 2000.

24. Keeley, Lawrence. War Before Civilization: The Myth of the Peaceful Savages. Oxford, UK: Oxford University Press, 1996.

25. Klein, Richard with Blake Edgar. The Dawn of Human Culture. New York: John Wiley & Sons, 2002.

26. Macdougall, Doug. Frozen Earth: The Once and Future Story of the Ices Ages. Berkeley, CA: University of California Press, 1994.

27. Masters, William, Virginia Johnson, and Robert C. Kolodny, (5th Edition). Human Sexuality. New York: Harper Collins College Publishers, 1995.

28. Minkel, J.R. Human-Chimp: Gene Gap Widens from Talley of Duplicate Genes. London, UK: Scientific American Magazine, December 2006.

29. Morris, Desmond. The Naked Ape. New York: Random House, 1967.

30. Newitz, Annalee. What Modern Humans Can Learn From the Neanderthals' Extinction. New York: Popular Science Magazine, 2013.

31. Niewoehner, Wesley. Early Modern Human Hand Remains: Behavioral Inferences from the Skhul/Qafzeh. Washington D.C.: National Academy of the Sciences, 2000.

32. O' Looney, Kate. Fire as a Symbol of Religion. Spokane, WA: Gonzaga University, 2012.

33. O'Neil, Dennis. Early Human Evolution. San Marcos, CA: Behavioral Science Department, Palomar College, 2013.

34. Prothero, Donald R. After the Dinosaurs: The Age of Mammals. Bloomington, IN: Indiana University Press, 2006.

35. Roberts, Alice. Evolution: The Human Story. London, UK: Dorling Kindersley Limited, 2011.

36. Roberts, J.M. and Odd Arne Westad. The History of the World. 6th Edition, New York: Oxford University Press, 2013.

37. Sawyer, G.J. and Viktor Deak. The Last Human. New Haven, CT: Yale University Press, 2007.

38. Seabright, Paul. The Company of Strangers: A Natural History of Economic Life. Princeton, NJ: Princeton University Press, 2004.

39. Stanford, Craig. Chimpanzee Hunting Behavior and Human Evolution. Triangle Park, NC: American Scientist Magazine, May-June 1995.

40. Stanford, Craig. The Hunting Apes: Meat Eating and the Origins of Human Behavior. Princeton, NJ: Princeton University Press, 1999.

41. Stringer, Chris. Lone Survivors: How We Came To Be the Only Humans On Earth. New York: Time Books, 2012.

42. Stringer, Chris and Peter Andrews. The Complete World of Human Evolution.New York: Thames & Hudson Inc., 2012.

43. Tattersall, Ian. Masters of the Planet: The Search for Human Origins. New York: Palgrave Macmillan, 2012.

44. Tudge, Colin. The Time Before History: 5 Million Years of Human Impact. New York: Scribner, 1996.

45. Vitebsky, Piers. Shamanism. Norman, OK: University of Oklahoma Press, 2001.

46. Wade, Nicholas. Before the Dawn: Recovering the Lost History of Our Ancestors. New York: Penguin Books, 2006.

47. Walsh, Roger. The World of Shamanism. Woodbury, MN: Llewellyn Publications 2007.

48. Wishart, David. Great Plains Indians. Lincoln, NE: University of Nebraska Press, 2007.

49. Wolpoff, Milford, John Hawks, and Rachel Caspari. Multiregional, Not Multiple Origins. Ann Arbor, MI.: Department of Anthropology, University of Michigan, 2000.

50. Wrangham, Richard and Dale Peterson. Demonic Males: Apes and the Origins of Human Violence. New York: Houghton Mifflin Co. 1996.

Index

F

Z